THE REASON WHY

True Stories of Past Lives, the Afterlife and other Spiritual Relationships

Debra Taubenslag

Published by Dove Keeper Press – USA
New Brunswick, New Jersey

For information contact :
Debra Taubenslag
http://www.debrataubenslag.com

Publishing Coordinator Susan Olak
Book and Cover design by Debra Taubenslag & Susan Olak

ISBN: 979-8-218-70455-1
LCCN: 2025912249
First Edition: July 2025

TABLE OF CONTENTS

About this Book

This is a three-part book. Part I is a memoir of how I spiritually awakened to other world realities through the eyes of my hypnosis clients. The stories are true, fascinating, sometimes scary, but utterly healing and inspirational.

Part II was written twenty-five years later and again, are true stories that teach spiritual wisdom. After decades of witnessing countless accounts of past life healings, after life communication, and connections with higher, lower, and lost beings; patterns emerged. These patterns I have come to acknowledge as spiritual truisms; learnings and teachings about our soul, spiritual growth, and of course, love.

Part III consists of Do-It-Yourself hypnosis, filled with specific scripts to discover your own spiritual identity, past-lives, connection to spirit, and various healing exercises. If you are called to explore; try them all. They are easy, fun and very insightful!

INTRODUCTION

I grew up in an open-minded, liberal Jewish household. We weren't religious but rather content to practice our own individual beliefs in God. As a young woman I had no opinion of God, one way or the other. It wasn't important to me. What mattered was the constant search in finding the right job, the right man, and the right lifestyle. I was qualified to be a teacher, but the idea of making a below-average salary was lower than the expectations I had for myself. So, I engaged in a variety of jobs to achieve a larger income. I was the file clerk in a music publishing company; I sold welding rods, non-asbestos building boards, textbooks, and dental supplies. Each position graduated my salary requirement but left me feeling empty and personally dissatisfied. I was like Pippin - always searching for "his corner of the sky." It wasn't until the birth of my son that my life began to change course.

What follows is a true personal account of my spiritual awakening to God and other realities. Some of the experiences are my own, and others are those of my massage and hypnotherapy clients who have taught me so much more than I could ever have imagined. For them I am eternally grateful. The accounts of the personal stories presented in this book come from either recordings or detailed notes of client sessions. The descriptions and the names of the clients have been purposely changed in order to ensure confidentiality and to protect their privacy.

Many of my clients had expressed initial fears of being the only ones with bizarre thoughts and feelings. But I knew that they weren't the only individuals out there looking for answers. How grateful they were to learn that there were many other people feeling the same restlessness and desire for something more. Working one on one (which I am sure is what God wanted me to do at that time) allowed me to synthesize all the fears and concerns that became part of my life and work. So why did I sit down to write a book about those universal concerns and issues? This hunger for spirituality is very prevalent; millions around the world are heeding its call. I know in my heart that I am most joyous and at peace when I am following my spiritual path. Maybe it doesn't (always) bring money, fame, or acceptance, but it always brings me a sense of well-being and purpose.

However, during those extended times when I forgot about my path; too busy worrying about monetary things or what other people thought best for me, my dog would somehow manage to literally stop me in my tracks. I have come to believe that writing this book was part of my divine plan, and something I was pushed into doing by my dog, Lucky.

One early morning in the fall of 1990, Lucky dug a hole in my back yard. I later tripped in the hole and sprained my ankle. Another time, Lucky placed his bone on the kitchen step which I overlooked; I tripped again and this time I sprained the other ankle. Both "accidents" kept me immobile. They literally put my life on hold! These events allowed me the luxury of time - to contemplate and finish whatever spiritual project I was procrastinating.

During the winter of 1996, Lucky, once again, stopped me in my tracks, but this time by attacking and ripping the flesh of my arm right off the bone. For days I sobbed because we had to put him to sleep. I questioned God, my angels, my soul, anyone who would listen, "Why did my beloved dog attack me?"

It wasn't until a year later that I received my answer. I was driving down Route 78 when I felt Lucky's presence. I didn't see him, but I knew he was with me; I could communicate with him. I sensed him licking my face and expressing that he didn't mean to hurt me, but that he had to do it. When I asked him, "Why?" I received an immediate (telepathic) answer, "How else would you have written the book!"

I felt goose bumps run up and down my spine. He was so right. I never thought of writing a book before. It just happened one day...I sat down in front of the computer to exercise my injured arm and hand, when all of a sudden, my fingers started typing out my story. I never wrestled with the words or had writer's block. The story just flowed like a river.

There are those who will doubt the validity of the following stories and realizations of the spiritual world. It doesn't matter if the reader chooses to believe or disbelieve, for we are all on different levels on the same path. If it feels comfortable and easy to accept, then you know you are ready to move forward in your personal growth. If it doesn't that's okay. Just reading about other spiritual realities can open your eyes to at least question the soul's existence. This is good. For it doesn't matter how long or which direction we take to reawaken to our pure spirit, all that matters is that we do.

PART I

SPIRITUAL AWAKENING

CHAPTER ONE

Psychic

*B*e careful what you wish for...it might come true! I remember sitting in the bathroom during "that time of month" thinking, "Am I always going to, have you? It's just not fair! I want, more than anything in the world, to have a baby; and you're just going to keep on coming. I wish you would just stop and never come back. But you won't...you'll always keep coming back because the doctor said I'll never be able to conceive; 'there's way too much damage,' he said. Oh, how I wish I could someday have a baby..."

These thoughts happened in November 1984. By mid-January I was very ill. I had already taken three sick days off from work. My head constantly throbbed like cymbals crashing out of beat; while my stomach flew around as if it was on a spinning whirlybird ride. I was nauseous and miserable! I assumed it was the flu. The family physician prescribed penicillin and told me to rest for a week or two. I didn't feel any better. I remember remember thinking about a heroine in one of Sydney Sheldon's books: a single professional woman who suffered from a horrible flu, later to be told she was pregnant. She had the same symptoms as I... She also secretly longed for a baby! I relished in the fantasy for about twenty minutes – until the phone rang. It was Patty, my sister-n-law, calling to check up on me. "You know, you're not getting any better. Do you think you could be pregnant?"

I, of course, laughed it off and told her how ridiculous and impossible that was. My boyfriend and I had been intimate, but I knew that it was indeed physically impossible to conceive. She made me promise that I would take a home pregnancy test the next day.

Why not? I had nothing to lost by doing so.

Well, you can imagine my surprise when I saw the blue circle! "Oh my God." I cried tears of joy. Immediately I picked up the phone to call my sister-in-law. She was as shocked as I was.

A few weeks later my girlfriend Cindy called to ask me if I wanted to go along with her to visit a psychic. She explained that the psychic was a medium who was able to talk with deceased loved ones and higher spiritual guides. What did I know about such things; being an atheist bordering on agnostic didn't prepare me for what was to follow.

As we approached the psychic's house, I felt uneasy but was amazed to see how traditional and homey it looked. The psychic was a female English professor in her forties. She worked at a nearby college. Her name was Donna, and she explained that she had a special gift to communicate with the spirits of deceased relatives. However, it wasn't until the last few years that she had finally accepted the reality of her ability and decided to encourage these feelings rather than deny them.

She requested that I sit quietly so she could scan my energy field. I felt a bit nervous and excited during this quiet meditation. She then began by saying, "I see an older man with a blue cap that has smiling blue eyes. He's lovingly saying that he is with you all the time. He stands next to you on your right side and wants you to know that he's only a thought away. (I knew immediately that she was talking about PA, my beloved grandpa who passed on almost a decade earlier.)

"On your left side is a plump, older woman who has light brown curly hair. She's of short stature. She says she is your grandmother on your father's side and wants you to know that the glasses you have been looking for are behind the washing machine. She is showing me a paintbrush and says that she paints her hair with it. She shows me this is a sign for you to know that it is truly her. (I was dumfounded...How in the world could she have known that!) Your grandparents are here today to prepare you for what is to come in the near future.

"First, you are carrying a male child. (I wasn't even showing...how did she know I was pregnant!) The status of the fetus looks healthy at this point, however, there will be a problem with oxygen. Know this...the baby will be born much earlier than expected. No matter what the doctors say, the baby will survive and turn out fine...have faith for it is part of the Divine plan." (There's something wrong with my baby!)

"Secondly, the father of this child will leave you to deal with the birth of this child alone. It's not that he doesn't care, he does. It is just that he is incapable of loving himself, let alone you. There is an intricate karmic connection between the three of you. In a former life, you were the father to both the boyfriend and the child. You favored the youngest son; the child you are to give birth to in this life, while mistreating the elder son, who is the boyfriend now. You have tried to heal the karmic relationship with the boyfriend but have been slighted by his inability to forgive old resentment and anger. Again, a familiar jealousy toward the brother/child returns. The spirits wish for you to move quickly out of your own resentment towards the father and concentrate your energy on the child within." (He can't really be leaving me, not now!)

"The spirits also want you to know that you will learn to love again. There is a man who will be a friend at first and we feel that it eventually turns into a romance. It will be a live-in situation at first and then turn to marriage. It will take a period of seven years since meeting this man before you marry." (Oh great...I'll be close to forty by the time I get married!)

Donna continued with many other details in my life, as well as specific messages from my grandparents to me and other family members. However, after hearing the distressing information in the beginning of the reading, my mind kept circling around trouble with oxygen, boyfriend leaving, and job in jeopardy! Needless to say, I felt really sorry that I had made this visit. My first and last psychic visit...or so I thought.

CHAPTER TWO

The Pact with God

"Oh my God, my back is killing me! My stomach hurts with such tremendous force. What did I eat last night! I can't believe I feel this sick."

"Debbie, why don't you give your doctor a call...my gut tells me you're in labor," said Grandma Kate (affectionately known as Nana).

"Nana, you really are worrying for nothing. Besides, I'm only six and a half months pregnant. I'm sure it's just gas or something."

"And I'm sure it's not. Please, do your old Nana a favor and just call the doctor. If it's nothing, then I'll just keep my mouth shut from now on."

So, to appease my Nana I reluctantly called the doctor. After all it was an early Sunday morning. I hadn't had my bagel and coffee yet, but I made the call because of Nana's persistence.

Well, Nana watched me like a hawk as I spoke with my obstetrician. She watched my concerned face whiten as my hand reached for my abdomen. "You see, I knew you were ready to deliver...I just knew it," said Nana reassuringly.

I was scared---not about having a baby prematurely, but about giving birth, because I hadn't started my Lamaze classes yet.

When I arrived at the hospital, the labor pains started immediately. I was full of nervous energy; I was like a kid waiting to be picked up by her prom date. My mom later informed me that all my girlfriends had organized to give me a super baby shower on this day; one which I'd obviously be missing. For a moment I felt really bad about not being there, but the guilt quickly left when the pains shot through me like a knife. "Mom this kid's coming out right now!"

There was no time for an epidural or any other anesthesia to alleviate the pain. I didn't know what to do except PUSH.

"Mom, if I had my choice to be with anyone at this moment, I'm glad it's you. Thanks for being here, Mom. Hey, where's the doctor? Are you an intern? Oh my God, I'm pushing with all my might. Is he out, is he out? Why isn't he crying? Is he breathing? What's going on? Is he alive? Oh my God..."

I don't remember anything after those questions. At this point, they knocked me out with anesthesia. Apparently, the doctors needed to go back inside me to find out why I gave birth at six and a half months.

When I awoke the first and only concern was to find out about Cole. (That's what I had named my son. Well, actually Nicholas, but Cole for short...after my beloved grandpa).

"He's in the intensive care nursery, but I don't think you're up to seeing him just yet," said my nurse.

"Well, you're mistaken, nothing is stopping me from seeing my son," I said defiantly. I put on a good show, but I was petrified at the thought of what I might see.

The intensive care nursery was ablaze with light and sound, many glaring lights and jarring sounds! There were so many tiny isolettes. They looked like incubators for baby chicks. The babies were so tiny. There were so many of them—twenty, maybe thirty. I kept wondering, "Where are all the mothers? Who's going to comfort these poor tiny babies?" When I finally found Cole, I was shocked by all the tubes and needles inside and outside his tiny little body. He was only three pounds and twelve ounces. A nurse approached me, "You know, this little guy is lucky to have so much weight on him. I understand you had gestational diabetes...that's probably what saved him. Guess it's a gift from God."

I was confused, because I didn't have that disease anymore, it went away the moment I gave birth.

"Gift from God, yeah right. If God was giving me a gift, why is he making my son suffer?"

She walked away and let me get acquainted with my son. I didn't really mean to have an attitude, it was just that I was so overwhelmed with an assortment of feelings: fear, gratitude, anger, and hope, to name a few. I didn't understand why my son, the son I had wanted for so long, was on the verge of death. There he lay lifeless in varying shades of yellow, blue and red. He would change colors depending upon his oxygen levels and stress. A respirator gave him breath, while a heart monitor registered is heartbeat.

A doctor approached me to discuss Cole's condition. He told me Cole's chances for survival were: "Slim, I'm afraid. And if by some miracle he does survive, he probably will be severely mentally impaired and never walk. The odds of these kinds of babies making it are very slim indeed."

I wanted to scream so badly that my lungs were aching for freedom of expression; I wanted to cry so badly that the knife in my throat was ripping it from ear to ear. But I didn't. I just looked down at my son and said, "Hello Coley. I'm your mom, and I don't know how I'm going to do it, but I'm going to get you better and take you home." I had no conscious idea why in the world I said that. Maybe I was in major denial.

My mind kept repeating what the psychic had said many months earlier, "No matter what the doctors tell you, know the baby will survive and turn out fine...it is part of the divine plan."

That psychic was right. Coley did survive. The boyfriend didn't, and neither did the job. It didn't matter though; all that mattered was spending my days and nights at the hospital with Cole. The nurses told me that my visits would literally make the difference between life and death, so I kept going. My son's recovery was anything but normal. He developed hydrocephalus (water on the brain) and numerous infections. Three time a day a resident would stick a needle, the size of a ruler, into his head to drain out excessive buildup of fluid. They never gave him pain killers or any anesthesia to numb him during this procedure. They said, "He doesn't feel it, it doesn't hurt him. Besides, we don't want to aggravate the already exhausted nervous system." It amazed me how I could watch this time and time again. Unbelievable, Cole never flinched. It was almost as though he was out of his body – like an eggshell, without the egg. They called this procedure "tapping." After the tapping, I would pick up little Cole and hold him close and sing to him. It was then that I would see my son come to life.

After two months, Cole had undergone two brain surgeries. He wasn't doing as wonderfully as everyone hoped. A staff doctor approached me about a new drug he was researching; he believed it had promise for Cole. "We have nothing to lose and everything to gain; all we have to do is stop tapping him to see if the drug will help him," the doctor said. I believed him. After all, he was a doctor!

Coley dropped down to under two pounds and his head blew up like a balloon. Something was terribly wrong. The doctor said not to worry, that it was a temporary setback. I was worried though, real worried. My gut was telling me that Cole was in trouble. That night I never went to sleep. I was so anxious. Soon the anxiety turned into downright fear and then a panic attack. "I'm freaking out and I can't help it," I shouted to the air. The uncontrollable sobbing made me shake and rock with intense force. I couldn't stop it. It was unreleased fury with no direction. I was losing control of my emotions and couldn't help it.

"Pa, Pa," I cried out. "Please help me, I'm so scared and frightened. I can't take it anymore. I tried so hard to bring Coley home healthy, but he's dying Pa. I just know it. He's dying because that doctor's treatment is killing him Pa... Pa... I need you. Oh God, I need you."

Just then, a bright, warm feeling came over me. It was as if a burst of sunshine had me in the spotlight. I felt warm, and safe, and profoundly loved. I felt arms around me, and knew they were Pa's. My shaking subsided into a slow rocking – just like when I was a little girl. When I was upset, Pa would sit me on his lap and rock me until I felt secure again. Pa was with me now, taking the pain away with his caressing arms and gently rocking. It wasn't until I was completely calm and in control that I realized that I had actually had a visitation from my grandpa who had been dead about five years. It was real, not my imagination. I know what I felt. I was powerfully awed by the experience.

It made me question all my beliefs about God. I humbly asked God if he really did exist? And if he did, I was willing to make a pact with him. I was not a religious person, but at that moment, I had found peace with thoughts of God. I swore to God, "God, if you save my child and make him whole, I will forever be of service to you. I don't know how, but I am sure that you will show me the way. This is my vow to you, my holy promise."

The next morning, I awoke energized, refreshed, and ready to defy the doctor's drug and his motive. My research found that without tapping, the fluid buildup in the brain causes scar tissue, which in turn causes brain damage. My gut was right after all! I consulted with other doctors and ordered the resident to tap Cole's brain once again. The consensus was that all my son needed was a shunt that would act as a plumbing system for him. With my ammunition, I confronted the doctor about his motives, and the potential harm of the medical treatment for my son and felt wonderful with my decision. I felt courageous because Pa and God were with me. It was the best thing I could have done because Coley finally came home three weeks later; shunt and all.

God saved my boy. But how in the world would I ever keep my side of the bargain? This service I promised was new to me. The last time I stepped into a temple was over a decade ago, maybe even as far back to the age of thirteen, when I attended a few schoolmates bar mitzvahs. I didn't know how to be religious. But something told me that the pact with God wasn't going to be about religion. I guess I would just have to wait for a message or sign of some sort.

CHAPTER THREE

Healing Energy

*C*ole's legs were stiff as boards. Every time I tried to bend them; an innate resistance would shield my efforts. His incredible rigidity called out for touch.

Day after day I would maternally massage his legs, hoping to bring relaxation to his muscles. Eventually they started to bend with the direction of my hands. It was as if they screamed out for manual attention. I was so overjoyed to see his muscles respond to my touch that I enrolled in massage school to learn more about the incredible world of touch.

Six months later a local health club proudly displayed my certified massage degree. I had no idea that this type of work would take me on an adventure...a spiritual journey that I never would have dreamed possible.

Many people booked appointments after their workouts at the gym, because they loved a Swedish massage on their sore muscles. I would dim the lights and play soft flowing new age or classical music to enhance the healing mood. While stroking their backs, I would find my knees bending slightly in order to sway with the movement of the rhythm. The swaying back and forth, along with the ambience of the room, soon pushed me ever so slightly into a trance.

While clients lay on the massage table, I found myself doing strange things. For no logical reason, I would lift my hands off the clients' bodies and start massaging the air around them. Sometimes it would be ever so gentle, like stroking an infant's back, and at other times my hands would flutter and shake fiercely as if I were chopping and breaking up ice. There were times when I would dance around the table like a Native American Shaman performing a ritual, and at other times I felt like a priest throwing holy water. There were instances when I wanted to make sounds so badly that I thought I would die, because my throat would get all choked up.

My breath was always deep, really deep. It sounded like the tide coming in at the seashore. I also felt strange sensations in my hands. Sometimes it felt light and airy, smooth and free flowing; other times it felt dense, sticky and mucousy. Sometimes it felt hot, or cold, and other times I felt electrical currents or cords that I could pull out of people if I felt an urge to do so. My clients must have thought I was bizarre. I couldn't help it, though. I never intentionally meant to enter into a trance and do such weird things. It just happened, time and time again.

One night, Jenny, a professional client in her thirties shared the following with me after her massage. "This was really crazy...I felt like I was floating above my body, and I could see you working on me. What's really weird is that I could see your hands on my abdomen, but I saw someone else's hands inside me. These hands were much larger than yours; and it's as if they were connected to yours but not really. They entered through your hands but ended up inside of me. And I could feel them as being separate from you. Your hands were hot. The other hands inside of me were moving things around. I could actually feel them moving and turning something, but I could not make out what it was. It didn't hurt, I could just feel the slight pressure and manipulation. It was unbelievable. If I didn't see it with my own eyes, I wouldn't believe it happened. This was really cool..."

Jenny and I were in shock at what had transpired during our session. I had been giving Jenny massages for quite some time and I never had anything like this occur before. Before her massage, Jenny complained of a splitting headache. You would have thought that The Hands would have gone insider her head to make her headache go away. We even laughed about why The Hands didn't get psychic enough to pick up on her current need. It turned out that indeed The Hands did. One month later, Jenny informed me that a cyst, the size of a grapefruit inside her reproductive area during the time of her last massage, had somehow miraculously disappeared. We both looked at each other and were in total awe of the situation. To this day I don't know why some people receive such incredible gifts of grace while others don't. I guess it's literally in God's hands.

This experience forced me into finding out more about trance movements, and all other strange feelings while giving a "non-touch" massage. Boy was I ever thirsty for knowledge! After reading countless books and attending numerous workshops, I soon discovered how common all of it was. The air I was massaging was the person's aura. There are many layers of this aura. The aura closest to the skin is known as the physical layer. Sometimes my hands would shake and twist one or two yards away. Little did I know that I was working on the emotional or astral layer. I guess I was guided to go wherever "priority" was.

I know that everything I was feeling was "energy." Sometimes energy was congested and needed to be broken up and freed, while at other times the energy was stagnant and needed to be free flowing. There were times when energy was sent from "God knows where" into a person's aura and being, for healing and wellness. When this happened, I always knew, because my feet would be firmly planted on the floor. It felt as if my feet wee roots that extended to the core of the earth. Even if I wanted to move, I couldn't. It was as if I were cemented to the floor. When it was over I would get a lightness in my hands and legs. Only then could I move away and shake my hands free.

On those nights something strange and wonderful would happen to me and everyone else who came in for a massage. Those clients only partially got what they came in for. They never knew what to expect; neither did I. All I did know was that I wasn't the one creating this energy. I know I was there participating, but I was not imparting the healing. I could always sense that there was another presence working through me. I can't explain it; that's the way it is.

This vibrating energy worked incredible wonders for my son Cole, too. He progressed steadily in both mind and body. I wasn't doing anything more for him than I was for my clients. However, he received more from this presence than I could have ever imagined. The neuro-pediatric specialists were baffled by his healing. All they knew was that he had measurable brain damage caused by a ventricular hemorrhage. The degree to which his brain was scarred produced unthinkable statistical odds. They continually prepared me for the worst outcome:

"It's highly probably that he will never walk due to the degree of the cerebral palsy, and his intelligence will probably be halted due to the mental disability." It's funny how I never took those sobering words seriously. I kept thinking about the psychic's advice, "No matter what the doctors say, the baby will turn out fine...have faith for it is part of the divine plan."

Well, my son has turned out fine! Nick (as he grew up, Cole decided the name Nick suited him better) is intelligent, creative, sensitive, funny, and highly intuitive. The doctors can't explain how the cerebral palsy, for the most part, disappeared. Nor can they comprehend how steadily his emotional and mental development has continued to progress. They call him the "miracle preemie," and are quite awed with his mysterious healing. Nick has come far but is not out of the woods. He still has to overcome challenges, but it is part of his "divine plan".

I have learned that everything truly happens for a reason; there are no accidents. I believe we all have divine plans: blueprints that are made before we are born. If only we could access our individual plans at will! I wonder how much happier we could be if we truly knew that there is a purpose to everything that happens to us. Some experiences are devastating, but each one always teaches us something if we are paying attention – something that our souls need to listen to, for our own awakening and healing. Well, needless to say, I am profoundly thankful to God and his energies for shing grace on Nick, and for waking me up from a robotic metropolitan sleep!

The psychic was also right about learning to love again. Dominic walked into my life as a friend; later he became my live-in lover. And just like she said, it took a period of seven years from the time we met until the time we married. To this day, it amazes me how she could have known that! I guess we really are destined; like I've said before...it's part of "the plan."

****

Just when I thought I couldn't be shocked anymore, I was struck by another incident that would change my life and push me forward into another direction.

Gail was a businesswoman in her late forties who came to

me for a stress-reducing massage. When she arrived, she had been quite tense from the demands of her day.

All she wanted was to unwind and relax. In fact, she relaxed so easily and deeply that she glided into trance before I did. I could tell she was in a very deep trance because her breath was really slow and deep. Her body was loose and limp like a rag doll, and she wasn't responding to my requests to roll over. She started talking, but to my surprise it wasn't to me. It became apparent that she was conversing with her mother who had passed on years before.

"Mom, it's good to see you too. I know, I know, (as she nodded her head) you told me this before. I know you didn't mean to hurt me. You couldn't help it. It wasn't your fault. You didn't know better. I don't blame you. (She starts crying.) Mom, stop it! Stop it! Just stop it! I don't want to remember. Leave it alone. Why do I have to? (She's getting really agitated.) I don't want to. It's not holding me back. Leave well enough alone. I forgave you a long time ago. Why do you bring this up now? But...What, how can you say that! Mom, you are really upsetting me! Go, go away. I don't want to talk with you anymore. Just go!" (She was crying really hard now and opened her eyes.)

I said to her, "Gail, what just happened? You were talking to your mother? How? Why are you so upset? What did she say?" I knew I had witnessed a very profound yet poignant experience. I wanted to know so badly about the details. In fact, I was dying to know, but I didn't have the right to invade her privacy. Just being there, I felt like an intruder.

But at that instant something told me Gail needed closure; she wasn't finished with her mother. So, I told her to close her eyes and breathe deeply. I then asked her to call her mother back because she had unfinished business. I told her I would leave the room out of respect for her, but she clung to my arm, and, like a frightened doe, asked me to stay and hold her hand while she confronted her mom again. I was secretly thankful to be privy again, and of course, did what she requested.

Sure enough, her mom came back into her mind's eye. But this time, Gail opened her eyes and told me her mom was in the room with us. When I asked her where, she said, "Right next to you."

I felt a cold chill move up my spine. Gail and her mom talked, shouted, cried, and made peace with each other in a little over an hour. I had heard and witnessed Gail's reactions. Unfortunately, I could not see or hear her mom's, only Gail could. It was as though I was an uninvited guest viewing and listening to a major confrontation and healing while the subject was on the phone. It was quite obvious that what was happening to Gail was real. There was no doubt in my mind. Only amazement.

After she left, I stayed in my massage room for quite some time. I had to figure out what had just happened. My client had a profound healing experience, and I was lucky enough to witness it. She cried in my arms with such gratitude and thanked me over and over again. I felt guilty taking the credit, since I knew I had nothing to do with it. All I did was relax her to a point of such profound relaxation that she drifted into a trance. Until now I thought I was the only one who naturally drifted into trance. Apparently, not! Gails's deep relaxed feeling sent her off into a place where she could access her mother.

Incredible! I had to find out how she got there. I had to find out more about trance.

CHAPTER FOUR

HYPNOSIS

*T*hat night, as I lay in bed, all I could think about was Gail and her mom. I couldn't sleep. Thought of trance, spirits, and massage haunted my mind with each breath I took. I pleaded with God to please help me make some sense all this. Finally, from sheer exhaustion, I fell asleep. The following morning when I awoke, I felt at peace. I had slept like a baby. My energy was incredibly high; I was exhilarated. I knew what I needed to do. I was going back to school to study hypnosis. By mid-afternoon I was enrolled and as excited as a kid going to the circus for the first time. The school was over an hour away; the class met twice a week for six months. I didn't care how far it was; I was going to explore the vast unpioneered territory of the mind.

Six months later I was certified as a hypnotherapist and ready to use my new techniques with my clients. I learned all about smoking cessation, weight loss, and stress management. I thought I knew it all; the wise advisor who could help those in need of my hypnosis talents. I was confident in my abilities because my clients told me how I helped them obtain their goals. Unfortunately, I was getting bored. There were very few clients who inspired me the way Gail and her mom had. Sure, I like helping people feel good about themselves, but something was missing. I needed more challenges. I wanted to be struck with a lightning bolt again. Jack was the one who did it for me this time.

I had met Jack a few years before, while working at the health club. Jack was a regular client. He would go into trance quite easily while being massaged. In fact, he was one of my favorite clients because he always shared his visual journeys with me. He knew I was involved with hypnosis and wondered if I could help him regain his photographic memory. Apparently, he had this remarkable gift as a teenager, but unfortunately it faded away after his eighteenth birthday. Now that he was in his late thirties (and a very successful businessman) he yearned to have that photographic memory back. He asked me if I could help him.

I said, "Well, I don't know, but I'm willing to try if you are. I can't imagine why you couldn't get it back. After all, it is in your subconscious. For whatever reason you turned it off. Let's see if we can turn it back on."

We booked an appointment for the following week. I gave him an assignment. He needed to meditate; to enter his subconscious to question himself, to probe his memory to give himself hints as to how he could regain this natural phenomenon. It was best to do this searching at bedtime. That's when the body and mind are more relaxed and receptive to requests and inquiries.

When he arrived at my house, Jack took a seat and was very excited about being hypnotized. I asked him to close his eyes and take long, deep breaths. Then I instructed him to visually and physically relax each individual part of his body. Once again Jack slipped easily into a hypnotic trance. I continued with the procedure: "Jack, now that you are completely relaxed, feeling safe and secure, and wonderfully at peace in this deep level of hypnosis, on the count of three, I want you to choose a moment back in time when you were easily using your photographic memory."

At that moment, Jack became stiff as a board. His buttocks rose off the seat of the chair while his neck arched all the way back as his jaw flew open. It appeared as if he were screaming his lungs out with all his might, and yet there was not a sound coming out of his mouth. I was shocked, and yet I knew by the contortions in his face that he was filled with rage.

"Jack, what is it? What are you trying to say? What is it that you can't seem to vocalize? Jack, can you talk?"

At this point I was becoming very concerned. I knew that he was going through a very serious crisis, and that I probably should have given him a suggestion to go immediately to a safe place and then end the session. However, intuitively I knew that if I did just that, he would have a lot of unfinished business that he really needed to scream about. I asked myself, what should I do?

The response came immediately. I was directed to get him paper and pencil. That's exactly what I did. I quickly ran into Nick's room to get paper and pen. Immediately a voice inside of me said, "Color - he needs to use color." I rummaged thought Nick's drawers and gathered all the crayons I could find and threw them down in front of Jack. His position never changed. His back remained arched, and he silently screamed his guts out.

I said, "Jack, draw your feelings. Draw what you need to say. You will open your eyes to draw, but you will remain in a deep trance. You will look at me and nod when you are finished. You will have complete comprehension and understanding of whatever you draw. You will easily interpret and verbalize everything to me."

Jack began to draw very intensely, and then he abruptly stopped what he was doing to carefully choose a specific color. He then proceeded to draw an entirely different object with an entirely different attitude and pace. It seemed as though there was music going on inside his head. One minute he would calmly be drawing to a waltz, and in the next minute his hands were swirling and gyrating with anger to a heavy metal beat. When I looked down at the paper it was as odd to me as modern art. Nothing made sense! The objects were unidentifiable, and there was absolutely no recognizable pattern. I would have to wait patiently until he interpreted the meaning of his drawing. I prayed that he would be able to do that.

Within twenty minutes he looked at me and nodded. Thank God! I was so curious. He pointed to a gold and green geometric shape. He said, "This is the tree where I sit and talk with the wise old man. He comes when I ask him to. He has always come. He talks about how I can help myself and offers advice to me in all areas of my life. I feel very safe and comfortable here. He is my special friend. I go to the tree once I am asleep."

So, I think to myself, this wise old man must be a guardian angel or something. Maybe he's just like Pa is to me. How interesting. "Go on please continue."

"This pink waterfall is a place I go when my spirit needs cleansing." Jack continued to explain, very matter of factly, all of the other symbols he drew. They all have to do with deep spiritual issues. He then went to the last object, which was a scribble in red and black. He immediately resumed that rigid posture and started screaming that silent rage again.

I said, "Jack, what is it?" What does the red and black mean?" Jack started shaking and perspiring. "Jack, tell me what is happening?"

He started shaking his head from side to side trying to say "no." He couldn't speak, but it was apparent that he was terrified out of his mind.

"Jack, go get the wise old man, the one who makes you feel safe. Get him and confront the red and black scribble."

The next thing I knew he started to verbalize all of his rage; screaming and crying, yelling at someone; he was literally verbally throwing up. When he finished, he pointed to the pink waterfall and then just said he needed a shower. I waited a few minutes not saying a sound; I didn't want to interrupt this sacred, powerful moment. He then positioned himself on the chair like a cat who stretches and finds his most optimum relaxed position. He opened up his eyes, looked at me and said, "Wow." His eyes appeared bright, and for the first time a profound peace had permeated his aura. He smiled at me and again said, "Wow."

When I asked him what happened he said, "The red and black scribble was my dad. I was terrified of him as a young boy. When I became eighteen, I left home and never went back. I didn't want to. Some things were best left unsaid." He cracked a smile and said, "Well, actually, a lot of things needed to be said, apparently!"

We both laughed and then he hugged me. I said, "What was that for? You went through hell and didn't get what you came in for. I'm sorry, I tried but I don't know why you had to go through what you did. I tried to help you recapture that photographic ability but that's not what you got, did you! Frankly, I really don't know what happened. I'm sorry."

"Are you kidding?" Jack said. "I had no idea how much anger and rage were pent up inside of me. I was hurting so hard and was only superficially aware of it. I guess this rage has been affecting all areas of my life; my relationships, career, friendships. Nothing was ever going my way. I always blamed it on others. How unfair life was to me. I felt like a victim all over again. I thought if I blocked out my dad all the pain would go away. But you see, it really didn't. It just reappeared in other situations in my adult life. I now know that I have to confront my fears, and then maybe they won't be so fearful after all."

He contemplated awhile, and then said, "Interesting - my photographic memory left me when I left my dad. I wonder what it all means."

He left feeling quite refreshed and rejuvenated. He expressed that he hadn't felt this light and at peace in a long, long time. I, on the other hand, was quite amazed and exhilarated by the session. I assumed the client's conscious request would be granted. Boy was I wrong! The subconscious mind went to what it considered priority. The subconscious mind was directed to go where it needed to go for the soul's highest good; and obviously not by me! With guidance from his guides and angels or whoever, Jack's higher self was the director. What a lesson! Amazing. I learned that I'm not the expert of my client, that his wonderful psychic self within is. We were both travelers on a journey. I'm just the tour guide, and the client is the traveler. We will travel wherever we need to go. My client's higher self will decide.

Approximately six months later I heard from Jack. He sent me a letter telling me that he had called and visited with his dad. They were planning to spend Christmas together. He also mentioned that he started to get his photographic memory back. How interesting indeed!

****

Immediately following my session with Jack, I enrolled in school to earn a doctorate in clinical hypnosis. Three years and many clients later God sent me Bill.

Bill's wife called me and asked if I could hypnotize her husband. She said that he had been out on disability for three months due to a numbing paralysis in his limbs. Bill was a technical engineer and was feeling hopeless and severely depressed.

"He was fine three months ago; I don't know what happened. He just lost all of his feeling in his arms and legs. He can still move around, but his limbs are numb. We've gone to every kind of doctor and have taken all kinds of tests. Now they're testing him for multiple sclerosis. He'll just die if they don't find out soon what is causing the paralysis. He is desperate. Do you think hypnosis could help him find some answers? I am just as desperate as he. This whole house has been turned upside-down, and I can't stomach the tension and depression anymore, you just got to help us, you just go to!"

I didn't know if I could help her husband, but I knew I had to try. I asked him to get on the phone. "Bill, I said, "if we're going to work together, I need you to start doing something for me. Before you doze off at tonight, I want you to tell yourself that you will remember your dreams. In fact, tell yourself that you want to have a specific dream about your problem."

To my surprise he agreed, and two weeks later came to see me with a tape recorder. He actually recorded his dreams upon waking, whether it was in the middle of the night, or in the wee hours of the morning. Bill was ready to work and get to the bottom of things.

"Bill, please take a seat in my recliner and make yourself comfortable. I'm sure you are a little nervous, but there really is nothing to be afraid of. You see, all hypnosis is really self-hypnosis. I don't have any control over you – that's just Hollywood. You have all the control. In fact, you actually control what suggestions you wish to receive and which ones you throw out. You will remember everything and probably wonder if you are really in hypnosis at all. That's because you are in an altered state of consciousness – not unconscious. Your body will feel deeply relaxed, and yet your mind will be a thousand times more alert than you are right now; you'll feel a heightened awareness while being deeply relaxed. Don't expect to go to sleep, because you won't. Any questions? No? Good, let's go to work."

I relaxed Bill by telling him to count down from one hundred. While he was counting to himself, I gave him verbal suggestions to relax each individual body part (whether he felt them or not) until I saw him physically start to "melt" into the chair. Then I too counted backwards to deepen his relaxation.

"Bill, on the count of three, you will try to open your eyes, but you may find that the harder you try to open them, the harder they remain shut; one...two...three. You see, you can't open them because you are so deeply relaxed, so deep in a hypnotic trance. This time, when I count from one to three, your subconscious mind will take you to the place where you can effortlessly retrieve information about your disorder. One...two...three...go to the cause of the numbness."

Bill's eyes began to flutter furiously and quite suddenly began talking in a high-pitched child's voice about his frustration with his mother. "It's not fair! My mother never lets me do anything. I wish I could run away!"

DT: How old are you, Bill?

Bill: Ten

DT: Why are you so upset?

Bill: Because she won't let me go. She's so mean. I want to go but I can't cause she won't let me. I hate her, I want to go, too.

25

DT: Where do you want to go?

Bill: To the game. All the other kids are going except for me. It's not fair. She never lets me do anything. She always says no. I hate her. (He's starting to get agitated, so I ask him to calm down and take some deep breaths before we continue.)

DT: It's okay Bill, take another deep breath. (Bill begins to relax.) Now would you like to continue...anything else you wish to tell me?

Bill: Yeah, I'm grounded again.

DT: How old are you?

Bill: Fourteen. She's such a bitch. I can't believe I can't leave the house until the end of the summer. All I did was stay out a little bit longer than I was supposed to and she goes and freaks out on me again. I mean – I can't believe it. I stayed out till 9:45 instead of 9:00. What's the big deal? She treats me like a baby – like a slave. She won't let me do anything. She never does. She has complete control over everything I do, I hate her. I really hate her. I should run away.

DT: Did you tell her your feelings?

Bill: What, are you nuts! Even my dad can't talk to her. Nobody can. We're all wimps around her. She controls us as if we were her puppets.

DT: How does she control you?

Bill: Well, she tells me that I have to live by her rules or find someplace else to live. But she is so unfair, she's strict, no she's more than strict, she's like a dictator who just bosses you around. She expects so much, too. She expects me to clean all the kid's rooms, feed them breakfast, and do my own chores before school. Then she expects me to do homework that she assigns as well as my own, plus hold down a part-time job which I hate since I have to give her all the money I earn. She's a bitch, I mean a real bitch. Do you know she has never told me that she loves me. I mean, I don't think I can remember if she ever even kissed me good night or told me that she was proud of me. (He's getting worked up again, but this time I let him go on. The tears start streaming down his face, and his words start getting choppy as his breath hastens and his volume raises. It is clear now that the frustration he had felt is turning into rage.)

DT: Bill, did you ever tell her how you feel? Did you ever express to her your needs for approval and affection?

Bill: NO. I never did. I couldn't do it even if I wanted to, because she wouldn't listen. She doesn't care about anybody. She doesn't know what the word love means. She's so cold and rigid. I freeze up just being in her presence. (He started to cry hard. It was apparent that his anger had been bottled up for a very long time. The crying was a release that was desperately needed.)

DT: Bill, picture her in your mind's eye. Picture her standing right in front of you now but place her in a bubble of white light. Now, tell her what you need to tell her.

Bill: Mother, I hate you. I always have, because you never let me do anything I wanted to. You always put me down and told me how I'm worth nothing; that I'm useless and that I won't ever amount to anything. Well, you're wrong. You're dead wrong. I have amounted to something and with no help from you! My whole life, all I ever wanted from you was to know that you liked me – that you were proud of me – that you cared. But no, you couldn't do that because you're such a bitch! Even dad can't stand you. Nobody can. All my life I wanted to tell you how I felt, how you smothered me, but I'm telling you now. Mother, go to hell! (Bill was crying his guts out at this point and was going through a catharsis indeed.) Oh my God, my fingers, my hands...I can feel them...they're tingling...Oh my God, what's happening?

DT: Bill, can you feel the tingling anywhere else? (At this

point, I was getting as excited as he was. I could not believe it either.)

Bill: Yeah, my legs are tingling too. Oh my God, I can't believe I can feel them. (His crying had changed tone now. Now they were tears of disbelief.)

DT: Answer the first thing that comes to mind...How is the numbness in your limbs connected to your anger towards your mother?

Bill: I numbed them, oh my God, I numbed them. I numbed them because I numbed my feelings. My legs and arms became numb because good sons can't get angry at their mothers. I couldn't express my frustration, so I numbed my emotions like a robot. But I had no idea how angry I really was. I guess it really needed to come out so somehow, I numbed my limbs. I don't know...I don't understand it. I don't know how my bottled anger could create numbness in my body, but I know it did. Somehow, I know there is a connection.

DT: The mind-body connection is pretty powerful, isn't it? Do you have all your feeling back?

Bill: No, just some tingling. (He's in a daze at this point; trying to take it all in.)

DT: Is there more?

Bill: Yeah...

DT: Well then, go on. Go to where you need to go, wherever that may be.

CHAPTER FIVE

PAST LIVES

*B*ill: This is really strange. I feel as if I'm floating out of my body, yet I have a sense of who I am. I'm in darkness, but it's not scary – it's kind of nice. I feel really peaceful.

DT: On the count of three, go to where you need to go – to the origin of the numbness. One...two...three...

Bill: I'm on a roof, building or repairing it. I'm not sure. I'm a carpenter, and I'm building a house. It's not my house though. I'm building it for Mr. James and the Mrs.

DT: Who is Mr. James?

Bill: Oh, he just about owns every good piece of land in this town. He hired Ben and me to build this here house for his summer home. We're almost done.

DT: Bill, what city are you in?

Bill: Bill...my name ain't Bill, it's John. John McBride. And I'm working in Cheswold, just a short ride from Dover.

(His whole mannerism changed; his tone and pitch of speech, as well as his body language.)

DT: I'm sorry, I didn't realize you were...never mind. (It was hard for me to understand what was happening. However, I knew I had to just keep going.) So, John, how old are you?

John: Thirty-six.

DT: And you're working as a carpenter for Mr. James.

John: That's right.

DT: What year is it, John?

John: 1769.

DT: (I was blown away...1769...incredible!) Are you married, John?

John: Ah yes, to the prettiest lass in all the county. Mary gave me four sons too, and they're just as fine as me. (By the look of his grin, he was obviously very proud of his family.)

DT: How come they are not helping you with Mr. James house?

John: Well, Ben is. He's my second. The others help their ma on the farm.

DT: Is there anything else you need to tell me before we move on to a significant event?

John: Yes, I'm a good builder, no I'm a great builder. In fact, I'm the best damn builder in these here parts. Probably the county. I can do anything with my two hands...and there is no man who could do better neither!

DT: Well, it is obvious that you are very proud of yourself. Are you ready, on the count of three go to the next significant event, one...two...three...

John: Oh God, no. No, no, no.

DT: What is it, what's happened?

John: I fell off my horse. My whole-body aches, and I can't move my arm. I think it's busted. Oh God, Jesus,

Mary and Joseph...how could I be so stupid! I wasn't paying attention, so I didn't see that damn tree lying down on the road. I think my horse's leg is broken too. Ah damn, damn... how the hell am I ever going to finish Mr. Jame's house now! (He's really worked up.)

DT: John, can you stand up? Are you able to ride your horse?

John: Yes, I'm standing now, but my horse can't ride, she's going to have to walk slow like me. Oh, what am I going to do now? I need that money that Mr. James was giving me when the job was done. My whole life depends on these here hands, and now they're as good as dead.

DT: John, it takes time to heal, you know that. And your arm will heal if you allow yourself the time to let it mend properly. Now, is there anything else you need to say before we move to the next significant event?

John: No, it's just that I feel so stuck. Only God knows when I'll be able to work. Hell, it might even take months!

DT: Well, it just might, but I'm sure you'll think of something to do in the meantime. One...two...three...move forward.

John: I'm at home with Mary. I'm a little older now, maybe in my forties. My beard is gray.

DT: How long did it take your arm to heal?

John: Not too long, about a month. My boys helped out a lot, they finished the job for me. I knew I could count on them. Fine boys.

DT: So, you got yourself worked up for nothing.

John: Yeah, I guess I did. (He chuckled at the idea of self-foolishness.)

DT: Is there anything else, John? If not, then go forward once again, one...two...three...

John: I'm floating over my body. I can see I'm lying in bed and Mary and the kids are crying all over me. I'm dead. But I'm not. That's my body, but it isn't me. I'm here. Can't they see that. I am trying to tell them that I'm all right, that I am here. That I'm really not dead. Ah, forget it...I can't get them to listen. I guess they'll see what I mean when it's their time. You know, it's funny being dead. It's not what I pictured it would be. I don't want to go back to that old body. It's sick and useless. I want to go to this light that I see. It's getting brighter and brighter. I am drawn to it. It's beautiful. I can't describe it, it's just beautiful. Peaceful and serene. I never want to leave it. But I feel like I'm moving in it...like I am traveling quickly, yet comfortably. Music too. I hear singing...I think...It's hard to describe, it just sounds so incredibly beautiful.

DT: Yes, John, your description does sound beautiful. Now ask the light to take you where you need to go.

Bill: I'm not John anymore, I'm just me. John was, and I guess still is, a part of me.

DT: What is the connection from John's life and your numbing disorder in this life?

Bill: I don't know, but when you just said that my arms and legs started tingling. (He's getting excited again; his speech and breathing are starting to accelerate.) I'm feeling them. I am really feeling them. I can't believe it. I'm really feeling my legs and arms again. Oh God, I can't believe it.

DT: Why are you feeling them, what is the connection?

Bill: I don't know, but I think it has something to do with John's injury to his arm and being out of work. Like me now! That's it! But I don't understand.

DT: It's okay, the answer will come when you are ready to receive it. Do you have complete feeling back?

Bill: No, but I can feel a lot more than I did before.

DT: Is there more?

Bill: Yes. (He's now drifting into a deeper state of hypnosis. I can see his breathing has slowed down, and he appears to be much more relaxed.) My wife Mary, in John's life, is my daughter in this life.

DT: How do you know that?

Bill: I don't know how I know; I just do. I guess I can see it in their eyes, or maybe I just recognize Mary's essence. I'm not sure how, but I do know for certain that they both are the same person; you know like John and I.

DT: That's pretty incredible! What a wonderful thought to realize that loved ones travel together through lifetimes; that we don't really lose each other through death but rather meet again when the timing is right. That's really a comfortable feeling. Is there anything else you need to say?

Bill: Yes, I feel I need to move on now.

DT: Well then, go where you need to go wherever that may be.

A few moments passed before he responded. I was feeling quite exhilarated by the experience and could not wait to see where he would go next. The fact that the past in another lifetime could directly affect the physical body of the present was truly amazing. And the fact that souls travel together life after life made my spirit soar, thinking that perhaps my beloved Pa has come back in one of my relative's or good friend's bodies. Just the thought of it made my eyes swell up with tears. I wondered if I would recognize Pa the way Bill recognized his wife. In those few precious moments, I began to realize how little we really know about man's psyche and how greatly it affects our whole way of life. My thoughts were then interrupted by a feminine inflection.

Bill: I'm in a kitchen stirrin' a big pot of soup. It's my job to make sure the family has their meals on time. I'm the cook of the house.

DT: What's your name?

Bill: Martha.

DT: Martha what?

Bill: I don't know, I can't seem to get a name other than Martha.

DT: It's okay, Martha. Whose house are you cooking in?

Martha: Oh, the Hendersons. They're rich people, with bratty children. One boy, one girl. The girl is my thorn – Gertrude's her name. Always in my way, fussin'and talkin', just won't stop. Needs a good lickin' if you ask me.

DT: Why do you dislike her so?

Martha: It's not just the little twit; the whole darn family is stuffy and spoiled. All they care about is their own kin. Nobody else. They walk in town like they were the queen and princess of it. I hear them gossip about everyone too. They always have somethin' nasty to say.

DT: How do they treat you?

Martha: Well, I suppose all right. I mean, he never hit me or anything like that.

DT: So why do you dislike them so?

Martha: Because they're stinkin' rich, that's why.

DT: But they gave you a job, and in a nice house, too. How long have you been with them?

Martha: Six years or so. And I ain't leavin' 'cause I got no place else to go.

DT: I see. Is there anything else you need to tell me before we move forward again?

Martha: Just that tonight is a very important night. The whole house is in a flurry 'cause that Mr. Lincoln is comin' to town. Mr. Henderson wants to see if Mr. Lincoln can come by the house for a visit, but we don't know yet if he is or if he isn't. The whole house has got to be looked over by Mrs. Henderson before two, so we're all rushin' around tryin' to get things just right.

DT: What year is it?

Martha: 1860.

DT: Now I know who Mr. Lincoln is. Is there anything else you need to tell me before we move to the next significant event?

Martha: No.

DT: Well then, on the count of three go to where you need to go; one...two...three...

Martha: Oh, dear God, it hurts...it hurts... (He's crying and holding out both of his arms, screaming, "It hurts.")

DT: You don't have to feel the pain. Rise above it and observe what is happening but feel your emotions. What hurts, what has happened?

Martha: My arms, I burnt my arms.

DT: What exactly happened?

Martha: I was rushin' to get things ready like I said, and before I knew it, knocked over the pot of soup...all over me. Oh dear, what am I goin' to do now. My arms are numb. They are burnt bad. The others want to help but they know they got to keep doin' their jobs to get ready. I go put my arms in cold water but the skin comes off. I'm in shock, 'cause I don't feel them. I mean, I feel pain, but I don't feel my arms neither. Worse yet, it's almost two and there's a big mess in the kitchen, and no soup! Oh, what am I goin' to do...what am I goin' to do... they'll throw me out, I just know it. No place to go, oh what am I goin' to do. (He's crying and feeling very concerned about his numbed arms and the future.)

DT: Jump ahead now, on the count of three, let's see how you made out. One...two...three...

Martha: I'm cookin' again, and I'm just fine. When Mrs. Henderson saw what I done she came and took care of me herself. She had the others clean up and someone else took care of the cookin'. Mr. Lincoln never did come over to the house, so it turned out okay.

DT: What about your arms? Did they heal all right?

Martha: Yeah, they did, but it took some time. A long time. I had to keep puttin' lard and herbs on them to make them heal better. They're ugly to look at, but I can use them. That's all that's important, I guess.

DT: Have your feeling changed about the Hendersons?

Martha: Somewhat, they're not as bad as I thought. Especially Mrs. Henderson. Never really gave her a chance. I suppose I was jealous 'cause she has a fine house, fine clothes and a husband. Everything I always wanted but never got.

DT: Is there anything else?

Martha: No, but I'm not Martha anymore. I'm Bill. (Apparently, Bill's higher self-directed him to leave his past life at this exact moment. However, I knew he was still in a deep hypnotic trance because of his physiological clues; slow deep breaths, limp posture, and slow speech.)

DT: Where are you, Bill?

Bill: Back here in the room with you.

DT: What are you thinking?

Bill: It's more like what I'm feeling. I can feel my arms

and legs again. There's more than just a tingling; it's like an itching – as if the blood is beginning to circulate and I can feel the current. It's a strange, but great feeling. I'm not home yet, but I know I'm close.

DT: Do you know what the connection was between Martha and Bill?

Bill: No, not yet. But I know I was her. Those were my thoughts, and my feelings. It's hard for me to believe I was a woman! I never dreamed that I could have lived before and be another sex! This is incredible to me. I want to work more, but not now. I need time to digest my new experiences. Thank you for awakening me to another reality. I don't understand it all yet, but I know we're getting there.

DT: You're welcome, but you know, I really need to thank you too. For I am learning all about this wonderful reality through you. On the count from one up to five you will reach full beta consciousness – back up to the full waking state, feeling totally refreshed, emotionally well and at peace, and spiritually uplifted. One...two...three...four...five. Wide awake, wide awake!

After Bill left my office, I sat stunned, exhausted and amazed. When I collected my thoughts, I contemplated for a very long time on what I learned from this experience: our past lives directly affect our present ones, our loved ones can travel through time with us, and it is possible to change gender in other lives. I wondered if there was a specific purpose in why certain lives came, and not others. I questioned if the past or possibly our present could have a direct influence on our future, or even future life. I wondered if Bill had a choice of a specific body, or if he was assigned to it. So many questions and thank God for sending me the work to answer them.

Bill came back to see me a week later. His whole outer appearance and demeanor had changed. Bill stood erect, his clothes and hair were well groomed, and he smiled easily – he was more relaxed and self-confident. This noticeable difference made me feel ecstatic. He had made remarkable progress. I was more certain than ever that we were headed in the right direction.

DT: You look great. How are you feeling?

Bill: Excited. My legs and arms are tingling – I know I'm getting the feeling back. I'm not home yet but I want to get the show on the road, I'm ready.

DT: Let's go then. (Once again, Bill relaxed in the comfortable recliner.) On the count from five down to one, go where you need to go, let your higher wisdom take you where you need to go – five...four...three...two...one.

Bill: I think it's the Middle Ages. I'm dressed like that period in history.

DT: Are you male or female?

Bill: Definitely male. I'm approximately twenty-five years old and grotesquely fat.

DT: What is your name?

Bill: I don't know. It's not important. What is important is the king's taxes. I'm the king's personal tax collector. It is my job to collect from every family in the kingdom. (He said this statement rather purposely but with an authoritative and pompous attitude.)

DT: Do you like this position?

Bill: It is my honor to serve the king in such a righteous manner, and I follow his commands without question.

DT: But I asked you if you liked it?

Bill: (He grinned cunningly and took a deep breath.) Yes, I like my position, I like the power. I like the way people squirm like rodents whenever they see me. This makes me laugh. I like the idea that they are afraid of me, it gives more power.

DT: Why do you need so much power?

Bill: I don't need power, I like it. There's a difference. I do not need anything or anyone. I like things the way they are, under my control. (He became agitated when I questioned his need for power; he was obviously more comfortable being aloof.)

DT: What are you thinking?

Bill: There's a farmer who's been lax in his payments to me. I have already warned him once before that he has to pay up or else he will lose the land, or possibly his life. The king doesn't like to be kept waiting. I have already charged him double for the double time I have had to wait. (He is laughing to himself and is quite amused.)

DT: What is so funny?

Bill: I've already had my way with his daughter, maybe I'll double that too, by taking his wife! (He laughs again, but now I understand the cynical tone behind it.)

DT: Why do you hate this farmer to such a degree that you had to abuse his daughter?

Bill: I don't hate him. He means nothing to me. He owes taxes to the king, and he didn't pay up. The daughter was there. Such a young fresh thing, I had to have her. So, I did.

DT: Did the father know you raped his daughter?

Bill: Of course, I made him watch. I told him that if he didn't watch, I would surely kill her as punishment for his disobedience to the king. As I raped the young one, my eyes burned into his. He needed to know my word was truth. I wanted him to fear me, and I succeeded. I have such power over these weak men. They are so meaningless. No spine.

DT: What would you have done if he tried to stop you?

Bill: Kill him, of course. (He looked at me with his eyes still closed – as if I had asked the most stupid question.)

DT: Is there anything else before we move to the next significant event?

Bill: No.

DT: Then move forward in time, one...two...three... What is happening now?

Bill: What a wretched bunch of fools. (Laughing that sinister laugh again) I torched them. Torched the whole house. When he couldn't pay up, I got mad. I lost my patience. He just stood there quivering like a sick woman. It made me sick just to watch his weak mouth pour out words of forgiveness and pardon. I couldn't listen anymore to the waste, so I had my men barricade them in, and then torch them up. What a pity I couldn't get the taxes for the king, but the king should be glad that at least I got him the land.

DT: How do you feel about what you've done?

Bill: I did my job. That's all that matters.

DT: Is there anything else, before we move forward? (He shook his head no.) Then let's go forward in time, one... two...three...With your mind's eye what do you see?

Bill: I'm old and fat. I'm dying of too much...

DT: Too much of what?

Bill: Alcohol. I've poisoned myself with too much wine. Oh well, I've done what I was supposed to do in this life. I served the king well, and I suppose I'm ready to die.

DT: Are you alone?

Bill: Of course, I lived alone, and I'll die alone. It does not matter.

DT: Then on the count of three, cross over to the light – one...two...three...

Bill: I left my body, but I don't see any light. Oh wait, I see something...it's a light but it's blinding me. Okay, I'm getting adjusted to it. It's penetrating into me, I can feel the light moving in and out of my body, as if it was a snake. Oh, I don't feel well. I feel nauseous, and faint. Ahh...sharp shooting pain in my groin...stabbing pain. Again, and again...I feel ripped apart! I am so terrified; I don't know what is happening to me. I can't make it stop! I have no control. Oh, my Lord, no it can't be. I see her, the young farmer's daughter. (His breathing is becoming loud and rapid. His breath is short, and he begins to shed tears.) I'm feeling her pain. It's like she's inside of me to show me how it feels. She's forcing me to feel it, and I can't stop her. I am feeling her fear, her anguish, and her pain. It's overwhelming and unbearable. Oh my God, no... no... I don't want to. I'm in the house and it's burning. All of them are inside me now. I can see and hear their internal screams; I hate this. I can't continue. Make it stop, please, make it stop. I'm choking, I can't breathe, help me. Please help me. (He's sobbing uncontrollably, hardly able to breathe from his own cries. I gave him a suggestion to breathe deep which enabled him to control his sobbing in order to convey his thoughts.) I'm sensing a panoramic view of my life now. I am experiencing everyone I ever caused harm to. I see and feel all their pain. Even the animals. I'm being tortured by their feelings. They are forcing me to bear witness to the deeds I have done. I'm in hell – that's what it is. But it is of my own making. I understand now. God, please hear me.

Please hear what I am saying. I am asking for forgiveness. Not because I want to stop the agony upon my soul, no. I understand that I deserve this. It is my punishment for my sins. I... I didn't realize how cruel I was until I felt their pain. I didn't think they mattered, but I was wrong. Oh God, I was wrong. We all matter, and what I did was dreadfully wrong. It was horrible, and I can't forgive myself, so I don't suppose that you will forgive me, either. How could you! I'm the wretched fool, for I broke all of your holiest commandments. (I watched Bill break into another bout of uncontrollable sobbing. I wanted to break in and tell him that he didn't have to feel it, but something was stuck in my throat. I couldn't get the words out; in fact, I couldn't move from my chair. I remembered from earlier sessions that when I feel stuck, it is intentional. I'm obviously supposed to keep my mouth shut, and let Bill go through his catharsis. I didn't interrupt him, but it was painful to watch.) I'm starting to calm down now; I feel the light changing inside of me. Something is leaving me... I feel it leave through my head. I'm feeling lighter now. Much more at peace. (A few minutes pass in total silence.) I'm surrounded by the most beautiful light. I feel only joy. It encompasses my whole being. Somehow, I know that the hell I experienced was of my own choice. God didn't make me suffer through that turmoil – my soul did. It wanted me to learn from that awful life I lived.

DT: And what did you learn from that life?

Bill: That it is terribly wrong to treat another human being or any living creature with disdain and disrespect. I possessed an inner evil in the names of greed, selfishness, and power.

DT: So how does this lesson fit in with the other lives you experienced, and the numbing of your limbs?

Bill: The agonizing pain I suffered while in my own hell instigated a sacred promise I made to my soul. I swore to myself and to God that anytime I would ever begin to show signs of those evil traits; greed, selfishness, and power, that my body would become numb as a warning to remind me of the past. My conscious mind couldn't remember, but apparently my soul does.

(I was struck dumb over the profound conclusions that Bill was able to obtain in trance. His desire to access his higher self for wisdom and truth confirmed in my heart that the client is truly the best and only source to solve his own problems.)

DT: What were you thinking or feeling; before your limbs became numb in this life?

Bill: I was jealous of my boss. I wanted his job. I was thinking of ways I could advance myself, gain more power with the company, not really caring if I hurt him in the process.

DT: And now?

Bill: Now I know better. I know I can gain empowerment by helping him. Being a team player, not a rival. (He opened his eyes at this point and just stared at me in amazement.)

DT: What is it, why are you staring at me?

Bill: I see colors around you. Blues and greens with some pink.

DT: Bill, come with me. (I rushed him into the bathroom and asked him to look into the mirror.) Do you see colors around you too?

Bill: Yes... I do. I see a beautiful hue of blue with some gold in it. This in incredible.

DT: What about your arms and legs? How do they feel?

Bill: I can't believe it, I almost forgot about them. I was

so mesmerized by what I was seeing in the mirror. My legs... they are fine! My arms and legs are fine! I can feel them completely. It's a miracle!

DT: It's not a miracle, Bill. You worked for it. You made a promise to yourself a long, long time ago. It took a lot of courage and determination to unfold the mystery and understand it all. But maybe you can change the conditions of your promise. Do you think that instead of numbing your limbs you can use a visual clue instead? What I'm getting at, is that all of a sudden you can see auras, including your own. I don't believe it is a coincidence. I believe it is your higher wisdom giving you and alternative choice to use for your benefit.

Bill: Yes, you are right. (He took a few deep breaths to quiet his mind and center himself.) I said a prayer, you know. I spoke to God during my vision from hell and knew I had to change the game plan. Now if I ever slip back into those negative patterns from the past, my soul has agreed to warn me by showing me signs in my aura. But I think I'm supposed to use my inner vision to help others as well. Yes, that's' it. That is what I am supposed to do. I'll help myself by helping others.

When Bill left my office, he was definitely in a daze of amazement. So was I! What we experienced was truly a miracle, initially. But what I have come to realize is that all of us are entitled to a miracle if we are willing to open ourselves up to our inner truth. What courage it took for Bill to awaken to other realities. What faith it took for both of us to trust each other and our guidance from God. What I reaffirmed through Bill was the law of karma, or in other words, the law of cause and effect. Bill's past life behaviors had a direct effect on the present. His higher wisdom made sure that he would learn from the mistakes of his past in order to balance and develop spiritually. What a beautiful thought to know that our lives have such meaning and purpose – that we are all here for a reason. The hard part is the process of discovering just exactly what are our life's lessons and missions. Fortunately, I was able find mine by helping countless clients find theirs.

In addition, many people have discovered hidden talents and gifts from prior lifetimes. For example, Bill was a fine carpenter in a former life. In this life he built a second story on his home without prior experience or knowledge. Somehow, he just knew what to do. Others discovered they possessed artistic, writing, mathematical gifts. This ability to tap into prior existences has enable people to explore other career options. Many clients have been helped when they witnessed and experienced their own success and accomplishments. They leave with a feeling of renewed vigor and commitment to seek out a career that will bring joy, rather than just money. They leave, not wanting to settle anymore. They want to do their life's work and are thankful that they were able to discover it for themselves.

Other people experience profound spiritual awakenings by God himself. They are only a few, but how fortunate for them to hear God speak directly to them. It takes tremendous effort on their part to remove emotional, mental, and physical blocks in order to experience a divine healing. Usually, they are unaware that they are ready for such an undertaking. I'm not aware myself. But God knows when the ideal time is, and that's when He appears.

****

One such person had no idea what she was about to experience. She came to me because she was curious. She had read about past lives and wanted to find out what it was like. Her name was Sarah, and her story brings tears to my eyes every time I think of it.

DT: On the count from ten down to one, see yourself walking through a museum of history. There are many exhibits, and you will be drawn to one in particular. Just allow yourself to be taken there by your higher self. It will be illuminated so you'll easily find the right one. Ten...nine...eight...seven...six...five...four...three...two...and now one... With your mind's eye tell me what you see.

Sarah: It's a saloon in the West. In the wild west days. I'm a beautiful girl. I have long dark red hair, with a slender yet curvy body. The men want me. I see them lust after me. I think I'm a prostitute.

DT: What's your name?

Sarah: Louise.

DT: How old are you?

Louise: About seventeen, maybe eighteen. I'm young, and yet I'm very old for my years. No, I'm hardened... I don't trust many people – men especially, that is. I mostly keep to myself when I'm not working with them.

DT: How did you become a prostitute?

Louise: I was on my own, there was nothing else I could do. I was cold and hungry. Lucy saw me and told me to come in and get something to eat. The girls were nice enough, and besides I needed a place to stay so I decided to try it out. It's not so bad, in fact it's quite easy...I just look pretty and lay there. Not much effort on my part.

DT: Is there anyone with whom you have a close relationship?

Louise: Well, there's John. He's the sheriff and my most devoted regular. He comes by to see me at least three or four times a week. He probably spends all his money just to be with me. He won't see any other girl, just me. He says he loves me, but I can't be bothered by it. It's nice and flattering, but I'm not interested in spending time with him outside...If you know what I mean.

DT: Why not? What's wrong with him?

Louise: Nothing really. He's got a pleasant face and a strong body. Not fat like some of the others. And he's real sweet to me – always saying nice things. Sometimes he brings me little gifts. I don't know, I'm not the kind of woman to run a house and have a family. I just don't want it.

DT: Has he ever asked you to marry him?

Louise: Yeah, but I want to stay here, in the house. I have my friends here. The girls are like my family. We have so much fun when we're not busy. And Lucy, I could never leave her. She's like, well...she's like an auntie to me. She's always watching out for me. I'm just comfortable where I am.

DT: Is there anything else you need to tell me before we move to the next significant event?

Louise: No.

DT: Well then, move forward on the count of three; one...two...three. What is happening now?

Louise: I'm marrying the sheriff.

DT: But I thought you didn't want to.

Louise: I don't, but I'm pregnant and I won't be able to work much longer once I start showing. I have to marry him, because he promised to take care of me. He's going to build me a house on top of the mountain. I don't want it. It's too far away from the girls. I want to be close to them, but he won't let me have any part of them once we're married. He says I've got a new life now, and I'll be happy if I give him a chance. He knows I don't love him, but he doesn't care. He thinks I'll learn to love him once we're together. I don't think so. I like him 'cause he's nice and all, but I'll never love him the way he wants. He's a fool to think I will, but what the hell...what choice do I have.

DT: Is it his baby?

Louise: How the hell should I know? Doesn't matter to him if it is or if it isn't. He says he'll be proud to raise it no matter what.

DT: He sounds like a very honorable gentleman. He sounds like he'll be a very good husband, too. You are actually quite lucky to have him.

Louise: Yeah, I guess so, but I just wish things were different. Like I said, I really don't want to marry him or any man, and I certainly don't want to have a baby and live like one of those townswomen who brush me off as if I weren't fit to live. But I'm stuck now, so I got to do what I got to do.

DT: Is there anything else? No? Then let's move forward; one...two...three.

Louise: John's away a lot. I'm home alone most of the time and I hate it. I'm very lonely and depressed. I gave birth a few days ago to a baby girl. Doc Peters came up to help me with the birth. John doesn't know yet. Somebody went to go fetch him. I hate it here. I'm truly miserable. I should have never married him. I feel nothing. Nothing for the baby, nothing for John, nothing for this house. (Her deadpan expression showed signs of a heavy cloud of apathy and lethargy.)

DT: Don't the girls ever come up to see you?

Louise: No, John forbade it. No one visits, not even Lucy. I want it to be over. (She paused for a few minutes and then sighed a long heavy breath.) It's done, it's over...I killed the baby.

DT: What! You killed your baby? Why? How?

Louise: I drowned it. I couldn't love her and I hate my life. I wanted out. I don't care anymore; I don't want to talk about it anymore.

DT: Is there anything else you need to tell me?

Louise: No.

DT: Ready, one...two...three. (Bloodcurdling screams shot out of her mouth. I watched in horror as her back arched up, and her face contorted in pain. With one hand she grabbed on to the arm of the chair, while the other held her lower belly. Sarah continued to scream while she tried to breathe. (My heart raced while I tried to console her. She wasn't taking my suggestions to rise above and observe. The only words she said were, "Doc Peters is making sure I never give birth again." She sobbed in pain for quite some time. When she calmed down, I was able to ask her what happened.

DT: Louise, I know that was extremely painful for you. You don't have to experience it again, but please try and tell me what exactly happened to you.

Louise: When John found out I killed the baby he went mad, really crazy. He made a pact with Doc Peters to keep quiet about what I had done. Doc Peters agreed on the condition that he would fix me. So, he did. He stuck something sharp like a knife, I guess, up me. I passed out eventually from the pain. When I came to, only John was there. He looked at me with sad, cold eyes and said, "I won't be coming back" and then he left. I never did see him again because he left town. I guess I hurt him more than I thought I would. Oh well, it doesn't matter. I told him that, but he wouldn't listen. Too late now, what's done is done.

DT: What did you do next?

Louise: I stayed on at the house. Lucy and the girls came to see me from time to time, but I was mostly alone. I preferred it that way. I didn't want anything to do with people, I just wanted to be left alone.

DT: How did you survive?

Louise: I went back to prostituting, but the men would come up to the house because I wouldn't go work in town. I made enough money to get by.

DT: And then?

Louise: And then died sometime in my thirties. I didn't want to live anymore, so one day I just took the gun and shot myself.

DT: I see... (I was exhausted and emotionally drained after experiencing Sarah's life with her. I know better than to get so emotionally involved with my client's lives...I couldn't help it though; this one pulled me right in. I couldn't wait until she was uplifted literally by the light.) Sarah, do you see anything?

Sarah: I see my dead body.

DT: Anything else?

Sarah: Oh wait, I see a light. It's a bright light and it's coming towards me. It's getting brighter and brighter but it's not blinding me. It's beckoning me to come into it...I'm in the light and it's beautiful. I feel so alive! So, loved! I must be in heaven.

DT: Well, I guess you are. What is happening now?

Sarah: Oh...Oh... (I watched her expression turn to complete joy and awe. All she could say was, "Oh.")

DT: Sarah, what is it? What is happening to you?

Sarah: It's God. God is with me. He's holding out his arms and showing me a little blonde-haired girl. He's telling me she's a gift to me if I learn the lesson.

DT: God! God is with you! What lesson does he mean? (Just then Sarah immediately changed her posture, expression and disposition. She shriveled up in the chair and cried like a frightened mouse.) Sarah, what's happened? Where are you?

Sarah: I'm Louise and I'm eleven years old, and I'm back in my stepfather's house. I'm afraid of him. He's mean, and he does mean things to me. (She starts to shake and cry.)

DT: It's okay, Louise I'm here. I promise not to let anything bad happen to you. You don't have to physically experience anything, but it is important to remember anything significant and tell me about it.

Louise: Okay. My mother died giving birth to my sister. I never met my father. I think he's dead, too. My stepfather decided to keep me, but he gave away my sister. He makes me clean and do chores for him. Sometimes I cook. But that's not all...He does bad things to me. You know, he makes me touch him in places I know I shouldn't. And sometimes he hurts me too; inside me. It hurts and stings and I don't like it. Sometimes he beats me when he's been drinking, too. A kid shouldn't have to go through what I'm going through. (She can't stop crying as she tells her story.) Anyway, one night he came home with a few of his friends. They were all drinking and getting really loud and crude. One of them sees me and grabs me on his lap. He starts grabbing my breasts and says I'm such a pretty girl. My stepfather laughs and agrees with him. Then my stepfather grabs me off from his friend's lap and pulls me down on top of him. He made me do things in front of his friends. I was so scared. I knew if I didn't do it, he'd kill me or hurt me, so I did what I was told.

When he was done with me, one of the other men wanted me to do things to him, too. I felt so bad about it, I just wanted to die. My stepfather pulled my hair and threatened me. He watched as I did his friend and joked with him how lucky he was that he got me all the time. When the man was finished, he slapped me on my rump and said that I was so good that he'd be back tomorrow for some more. (The sobbing was so intense that I thought I should stop her, buy my voice was nowhere to be found. I couldn't even get a peep out. It was as if I were being prevented from speaking. I wondered if it were God who initiated this lack of response from me in order to ensure a catharsis for Sarah.) I just couldn't go through it again, not ever. So that night, when my stepfather was asleep, I packed up a change of clothes, some food, and stole some money. I ran away. I ran all night. I slept a little and then kept on going. I eventually came upon a railroad and followed it into town. When a train stopped, I snuck on. I got off when I woke up. I had no idea where I was. I just knew I was far away from him and that's all that mattered.

DT: Yes, I understand. You did what you had to do. Go on, what happened next?

Louise: I walked into town. It seemed like a nice town because people smiled at me even though they didn't know me. But I was cold and hungry. I needed to find a place before the sun went down, so I went asking about for a job. No one had work for a girl who looked sickly and weak. I didn't know what I was going to do, so I just sat down and started to cry. That's when Lucy found me. I stayed with her and the girls until I married.

DT: How did it feel to be a prostitute after all the abuse you went through?

Louise: I felt in control. Besides, I was loved by the girls and some of the regulars. I felt like I had a family for the first time.

DT: And now...how do you feel now?

Louise: (She thought for a while before responding.) Relieved. Like a black cloud has risen off my heart. I don't hate myself for killing my baby anymore. I understand now. I killed her to spare her great misery and abuse. I didn't want her to experience what I had. My own painful childhood distorted my reality. The guilt and shame I had carried was horrendous. What I did was a terrible thing. But I was mentally and emotionally disturbed. I can forgive myself now, because I understand and can recognize little Louise's pain. I ignored it. I dissociated from her. I refused to acknowledge that she even existed. It was easier that way. Her cries were buried deep inside and didn't surface until I gave birth to a baby girl. Like I said, I understand now, and it's strange but I actually feel comforted with this knowledge. I have a sense of peace now that I wasn't ever aware of before. I feel okay inside my body. I feel an acceptance that I could not ever feel before. Do you understand what I'm saying?

DT: Yes, Louise, I do. Is there anything else you need to say?

Louise: Only that I see God again. He's smiling and showing me the little blonde-haired girl. What do you think it means?

DT: I don't know, only you can answer that...Why don't you ask him?

Louise: I just did...he just smiles. Oh, wait! Oh my God, I know what that little girl means. (She starts crying again, but with tears of joy rather than pain.) That girl is God's gift to me like he said. I thought it was me recapturing myself. Maybe that is partly true, but it's more. She's a gift to me in Sarah's life. I can't believe it. Oh God... (She's crying heavily now.)

God, thank you.

DT: What is it? What did you realize? (I was getting very anxious and excited by her response. I couldn't wait to hear what she had to tell me.)

Sarah: My husband and I have been trying to have a baby for over nine years. We just about gave up. I think she's mine. Oh God, I hope so.

DT: (When her crying slowed down enough to catch her breath, I had her breathe long deep breaths before we continued.) That's incredible, Sarah. What do you believe is the connection now between Louise's life and yours?

Sarah: That maybe my inability to conceive had nothing to do with physiological reasons. That maybe my psyche was blocking me from having a baby. Thay maybe I forbade myself to have a baby because I murdered her in Louise's life. (She paused for a very long time.) Maybe I needed to forgive myself before any healing could take place. You know, I used to blame God for my infertility. Now I think I was the one who put the barrier up in the first place. God wants me to have a baby. He told me she's mine, but I had to learn the lesson first. Oh, do you really think I'm healed? Do you think this is all true? (She opened her eyes, took a deep breath and then stared at me.) Is it real? (She paused again for quite some time then looked at me with hopeful eyes.) Where did it all come from?

DT: Well, I genuinely believe that what you experienced is your own personal truth. As for where it came from...I think only you can answer that. Do you believe you made it up? I don't think you did. It was too intense, too emotional for you to just create a fantasy like that out of thin air. Even if you did, what would have been your motivation to do so? Why on earth would you want to go through a physical and emotional trauma just to fool me or yourself? What would be the point? This is only my belief. What's important is what you believe.

Sarah: I don't know what to think...I want to believe so badly that's it's all true, but it's all so foreign to me. I came here out of curiosity, but I found something so much more. It's funny, but I feel exhausted and exhilarated at the same time. I have a lot to digest. Thank you, and I hope with all my heart that this was real...

I never saw her again. Oh, she sent plenty of referrals, but Sarah never came back to tell me if anything changed in her life. I was always curious but respected her privacy. Fortunately for me, I found out quite innocently from a referral a year later that Sarah indeed had a baby girl. When I heard the news, chills ran up and down my spine. God, how I love this work!

CHAPTER SIX

PERSONAL JOURNEYS

*T*here comes a time when you just have to practice what you preach. Here I was conducting countless healing sessions for other people and ignoring my own inner cries. I know what my clients call the safety zone...it's much more comfortable being unaware than growing in spiritual development. It was time for me to concentrate on me. I knew I had work to do, because I was feeling those unexplainable blues. Of course, we always blame it on our moods or hormones, but I knew better. These feelings were something more that my higher self-wanted me to look at, so I did. I met with a fellow hypnotist who believes that there is also a spiritual side to life. My first session produced an array of unexpected characters; and a series of past lives. I saw myself as a pitiful spoiled Southern grandmother who was rejected by her son and daughter-in-law, a frustrated Native American medicine man who procrastinated the feat of constructing a totem pole to initiate war with a neighboring tribe, and a jealous ancient Chinese male who murdered his brother for spite. My ugly past history took me by surprise, but I understood that everyone has a light and dark side.

This initial session gave me the chance to experience what my clients had been experiencing. My primary mode of receiving information was kinesthetic. I would feel things so intensely; I would have a sense of just knowing. Sometimes flashes of visual pictures would come to mind, and sometimes the words would just pour out of my mouth. There was never any kind of conscious thought to what I would say, it would just happen. Many of my clients would tell me that they saw whole scenes quite vividly, or that they clearly heard their own voice or others speak to them. I, on the other hand, received visual and auditory messages, but primarily felt intense emotions. These kinesthetic feelings were my higher self's choice to assist me in absorbing whatever it was I had to experience for my highest good.

While processing my past lifetimes, I realized that each life had a profound effect on my present life. I too was recreating patterns, blocks, or desires due to past life experiences. In subsequent sessions I relived lives as a male Polish immigrant who abandoned his wife and children for the good life in America; I became an African native youth responsible for the care of his younger brother; and I was a farmer's widow who gave up her kids in order to work to save her farm and in time realized that she would never see her children again.

These lifetimes were emotionally and physically painful, but necessary to relive in order for me to have a catharsis and for healing to occur. I knew that if I didn't work through these spiritual blocks, I would end up hindering my development and probably create some physical manifestation in my body that would not be pleasant. I thanked Pa for helping me to see that I too needed to clean house in order to move on with my life. Fortunately, not all of the lifetimes were unpleasant. Some, in fact, were richly rewarding and supportive to the work I do now. This helped me profoundly, because it reconfirmed that I was doing what I was supposed to be doing (in this lifetime) - that I was following my divine plan.

In most cases, I recognized someone I know now in this life. I have been given the chance to get it right with them, or the karmic ties that bind us are so loving and strong that out of pure joy we wanted to be together again. This is what I call chemistry; two old souls reuniting. In either case, it reminds me of the spiritual truth that souls travel together over and over again for specific reasons, either for love or lessons.

We are here to develop our souls, to become as Christ-like, Moses-like, Buddha-like, Mohammed-like as possible. This is our school. It is here, in the physical body that we learn how to love our fellow man, all of God's creatures and, most of all, our selves. Some of us are very old souls who have taken many lifetimes to learn our lessons, while others are just starting out. We reincarnate in specific circumstances in order to facilitate our growth. This is why we choose our parents. They are able to provide us with the exact opportunities we need in order to fulfill our soul's requirement. Life is like our school system: some enter at kindergarten, while others go straight to high school. That is why, in my opinion, there are no low life's in our society but rather low levels. These souls haven't learned the meaning of self-worth and their connection to God. They haven't a clue as to how their actions will directly affect their present life – and lives to come. They haven't understood the reality of karma and how it can either hinder or help.

Through my work, I've been able to conclude that we all have the ability and opportunity to progress...if we really want to. The awakening occurs when the soul humbly asks for it.

CHAPTER SEVEN

SELF INDUCED PHENOMENA

A few years passed. Again, I felt that familiar pang of inner work calling out. I was depressed, anxious irritated... nothing was making me feel settled. I have repeatedly told my clients that when they have felt such emotions, it's actually a wakeup call to the soul – a warning. Our higher self is trying say, Wake up! It's time for growth. You're miserable because you're aching to expand your horizons. Be wise and realize that your negative feelings are a sign that you are not in harmony – that you've become stagnant and thrown off your course. Thank them for being your alarm and let them know that they no longer need to ring, because you have awakened and are now ready to take action. How easy it is to tell others; how hard it is to practice what you preach.

One day I was so miserable that I humbly asked God to help me rid myself of these terrible negative feelings. I was alone and felt comfortable to pray for divine help. What then occurred took me by surprise. I was seated at the edge of the bed. Suddenly my back dramatically arched and my lower abdomen protruded forward. My legs flew open, and I had the strangest feeling I was about to give birth. My breath quickened, and my heart was pounding a mile a minute. "My God," I thought, "what's happening?" Fear started to creep into my veins, but something inside told me to just go with it.

My belly became extended, and my body perspired profusely. My cheeks became stained with mascara because I couldn't stop sobbing. No words came to mind, just feelings of intense grief and pain. The ache in my chest was so profound I thought I was going to die – not from the experience but rather from a broken heart. No matter how hard I tried to stop the inner pain, the stronger it flowed. My conscious mind was thinking, "This is really weird, you've flipped..." but my subconscious mind was saying, "Allow it to happen, just continue and let go..." The fear began to settle once I began to realize what was really happening. Though it was emotionally gut wrenching, I had found myself thinking, "How lucky I am to experience something new firsthand." I allowed it to continue. As I started to feel a strange sensation move from my groin, I jumped right in to participate, in order to truly benefit from this strange experience. As soon as I agreed to accept the experience, my psychic faculties took over. I actually transformed into a young maiden wearing a long skirt, that was hiked up over my shoulders. I was alone, in the woods, and giving birth. I continued to wail and sob profusely, because I knew that baby, I was birthing was dead. The lifeless infant lay still as I cradled it close to my heart. I too lay still as I curled up on the forest floor thinking it would bring me comfort. I somehow knew that I was kicked out of the master's house and had no place else to go. I also knew that it was the master who had taken me to his bed and now wanted nothing more to do with me. I was alone in the world and the baby was the only thing that kept me living. Now that it was dead I wanted to die, too. So, I continued to just lie there praying that God would send the angel of death to me.

Quite some time passed before a middle-aged man appeared. He was dressed in a hunter's garb. I could sense his eyes upon me, and before I knew it, he had picked me up and carried me off. I didn't care who he was, or where I was going. I didn't scream, fight, or try to get away. I couldn't, even if I wanted to, because I was too weak and couldn't walk. As I said, I just wanted to die. I don't know what happened to my baby...all I do know is that I stayed on with this man until the end of my life. Then, without warning the scene vanished. I was back sitting on my bed and totally shocked at what just transpired. It took a while to regain my composure, and when I was fully able to breathe again, I had an uncanny urge to get a flower bulb. The thought was so commanding that I actually got in my car and drove to Home Depot to buy a tulip bulb. When I got home, I immediately went into my forest-like backyard, hunted for the right stump, and buried that bulb. As I dug my hands into the earth, I cried and cried as I mouthed the words aloud to the Lord's Prayer. But, at that moment I knew it thoroughly, and spoke it from my heart.

After I knew my work was done, my eyes caught my hammock...it lured me to rest. Needless to say, I was physically and mentally exhausted and didn't have the energy to figure out what exactly had just happened. Within seconds I was fast asleep. When I awoke, I had that strange urge to go back into my bedroom...something told me I wasn't finished.

As I sat myself on the edge of the bed, I took a few deep breaths and said, "Okay God, I'm here. I'm wiped out, but I'm willing to go further because I feel the tingling inside my body that's telling me to work. I'm not sure if I can handle anymore, but apparently you think I can, so let's go for it!" Suddenly I was thrust back by an unexplainable force. It spread my legs wide open and held my arms pinned down. The only thing I could raise was my neck. The fear that welled up was nothing compared to the rage I felt. The screams that were coming out of me were so inhuman, like an animal being ripped open from the inside out. This time the sobbing was not cries of wailing but rather came from intense frustration and hate.

I didn't feel any physical pain, other than a strong pressure in my heart. However, the emotional pain was severe because at that moment I knew I was being raped by more than one man. I could see and feel the presence of the male figures, sneering and snickering at me as if I were a quivering little rabbit. "I hate you; I hate you," I screamed. My torso thrashed back and forth, trying desperately to free myself from their grip. Even the veins in my neck screamed from the strain of pulling my body up.

The more I tried to fight, the more they laughed at my efforts. I really did hate them. At that moment I wished them all dead. I wanted to kill them myself and make them suffer a slow death like they were torturing me. My screams continued until the vision disappeared. When it was all over, I just laid there numb. Yes, I was utterly exhausted; at that moment I had very mixed emotions about the experience; rage was mixed up with compassion. I started to cry softly for the poor girl who suffered so greatly; wanting to comfort her, to let her know it's over – to let her know that she doesn't have to carry the rage in her heart anymore. But I didn't know how to let go of it, so I asked God to help me. "God, I didn't know there was so much hate inside of me. I couldn't have ever imagined that a person could hate as much as I did. It so bad; these horrible feelings. I want to get rid of them, but I don't know how. Oh God, please help me release it from my body. Please help me release it from my heart, and my soul. I don't want it anymore. Help me to let go of it."

I cried and cried. But this time, the most amazing thing happened. I stepped outside of my body and watched the physical me release the anger through my tears. I remember thinking, "This is incredible. Part of me is having a catharsis while the other part is watching sympathetically – but with detachment. Thank you, God, for giving me the chance to cleanse my body and soul, and for taking out the garbage that's no longer wanted."

A few days passed. This time allowed me to gain some energy and process what transpired. Prayer always helped me before, so I felt comfortable just asking for assistance. "God, what was it that you wanted me to learn?"

Just then a voice from within me said, "You needed to recognize where your fear of intimacy came from. Until now, you have lived partly alive. You may think that you have lived a full life, but that is only partially true. You have loved only those you consider safe. These souls you know very well because you care and listen well, but the love is lopsided because they hardly know you. What you consider private is really a protective coating that blocks other's light into your heart.

"When someone gets too close, you listen to the siren of the past that warns of danger. How unfortunate, because you have missed out on so many opportunities of pure joy and enlightenment. It is time for you to learn the truth about yourself: you are a deserving soul...you are worthy of love. It is that simple.

So, wake up now, and realize the burden of despair is off your shoulders. You are free to open your heart again. And should your path connect you to souls who mean to do you harm, understand that they know not what they do. You are wiser now. For you know that resentment, anger or fear will only cause destruction for you and not for them. They are on their own paths and will initiate karmic experiences from their actions. You will do the same, depending on your thoughts and actions as well. Now you are enlightened, which path are you going to take? The familiar one that offers safety but spiritual depression, or the path that leads to love like you have never known. Follow the light – for you will always be guided with a loving hand."

****

    I contemplated how true it all was. I was dumfounded and beyond words. Exhaustion had turned into exhilaration. I couldn't wait to tell my husband, because I had never opened up and shared with him my deepest thoughts and feelings before. I was always too afraid and mistrusting. Not just with him, but with every man. Now I understood why. I couldn't wait to see how this experience was going to change our relationship. I wondered if he realized how much he was missing from me too. My thoughts were racing, but I turned them back to God and said, "Thank you for showing me what I needed to learn. Is there anything else?"

    And God said, "Yes. Now you are able to truly heal your clients, for you have walked in their shoes." Talk about a humbling experience...

CHAPTER EIGHT

ANGELS AND OTHER SPIRITUAL BEINGS

*O*ver the years, I have been fortunate enough to come in contact with all kinds of angels and spirits through my client's encounters. The spiritual beings are as widespread and diverse as my clients. No two have appeared alike in the same manner or appearance. Such varied descriptions range from reports of a color of light, for example a blue light, while others are visited by an old wise man or woman in an ancient looking robe. Still others witness an ordinary looking person dressed in professional attire but know they are not of this earth. All the beings may appear to us in different forms but the one thing they have in common is the genuine concern and love for the person they are visiting.

Some of the spirits come to offer advice on day to day living; some come to advise on spiritual matters; some come to join us on the spiritual past life/future life journeys; and others come to comfort and offer solace. I never know what's going to happen and how, but it is always an awakening for both the client and me.

I like to call the spiritual beings "teachers" because we learn so much from them. The following descriptions are my own beliefs based on encounters with numerous teachers. Some of the teachings came through clients, while others came from personal experiences while in trance, meditation, and actual visitation.

What I learned first is that there is a definite universal order with a specific hierarchy of angels and spirit guides. From what I've been taught, each human being is an energy of light that vibrates at a specific rate, depending upon what level we have achieved in our development. Our physical body is just an eggshell. It houses our soul for this lifetime of lessons. We are not physical beings trying to be spiritual, but rather spiritual beings trying to be physical! Once we leave the body, we are free from its entrapment and are able to develop our spiritual growth in an easier form. How we do this is quite simple: by helping others. It was Edgar Cayce who said, you will not enter the kingdom of heaven, except leaning upon the arm of someone you helped.

So that's what spiritual beings do...they help us. And by helping us they help themselves attain higher levels. The lowest level is darkness. Those souls who we say are evil are actually souls who have complete void of light; they refuse to acknowledge the existence of God and love, and are therefore blinded by their own darkness. Lucky for them there are spiritual helpers who will try to assist them if they choose to wake up and see the light. These helpers have been assigned to these souls because they have just awakened themselves, so their vibrations are somewhat higher than those they help.

Angels, on the other hand, have never been in body. They vibrate at their own rate and are here to watch over us and keep us out of harm's way. When I asked, "Why then do accidents or deaths occur?" they have stated that it was part of the soul's karma, their divine plan which cannot be disrupted by anyone other than self or God. With regard to death, they explain that one, two, or many angels come to greet the soul in order to assist with the transition. They come out of pure, unconditional love for us. It is their job and their passion to do so.

I once met an angel on a street corner, though at the time I didn't know it. I was walking out of a dentist's office when a tall, black man wearing a delivery uniform followed me out from the same office. He greeted me with "Hello," when we reached the street and said, "You're aware of the light, aren't you?" Even though he asked me a question, he said it with a matter-of-fact tone. When I looked up at him, my head had to arch back, for he was incredibly tall. His eyes smiled brightly, and I kept wondering why in the world this stranger had approached me, and with such a question! So, I innocently replied, "Yes, I suppose I am. Why do you ask?"

And then he paused for a moment, and said, "There will come a time when you have to say the following words to someone. You will know when the time is right, for you will just say them. Listen carefully now, to the words you are to speak: "Sometimes you have to hit rock bottom before you can rebuild.""

I just looked up at him again, and said, "You're kidding, right.... that's it? And who am I supposed to say this to? How will I know when the time is right? And who are you anyway?"

The tall man replied, "As I said, you will know when the time is right. I am a messenger." He laughed while he pointed to a delivery truck parked in the street. Then he tipped his hat, and said, "Good day."

I was really amused by this encounter, and yet curious about it because, let's face it, how many times does a man approach you and tell you to recite some words to whomever and whenever? I wondered who he really was, so I returned to the dentist's office and asked the receptionist if she knew the name of the tall, black man who made a delivery to her a few minutes ago.

She looked at me strangely and said, "A tall, black delivery man? No, I'm sorry, but no one who fits that description has come into this office today. We haven't received any deliveries, either."

I became a little assertive with my questioning. "Are you sure? He walked out of the office, right behind me."

"Yes, I'm quite sure, because I'm the only one here at the front desk and I have not left it for nearly two hours."

I thanked her and left. I was really confused. I was certain that she just must have missed him, but I couldn't see how since his height was so astonishing!

That night, a client whom I had seen a number of times before was rambling on and on in hypnosis about her alcoholic husband who had been clean and sober for over two years. She had a very difficult time forgiving him for all of the grief she struggled through during his addiction. Even though he is wonderfully supportive, loving, and trustworthy to her now, she still is bitterly angry and is considering divorce. Normally I am very focused on the client, but maybe because she rambled on and on, I drifted off myself. Suddenly an energy came inside and pushed me right out of my chair. Without knowing, I placed my hands upon her shoulder and shook her awake firmly and said, "Sometimes you have to hit rock bottom before you can rebuild."

She just stared back at me with an incredibly awed expression, and said, "You're right."

I stared back at her and said, "Huh? What did I just say?"

And she said, "Sometimes you have to hit rock bottom before you can rebuild."

And I said, "You are not going to believe this." I proceeded to tell her about my encounter. We were both awed and truly inspired by the experience (not a coincidence) that obviously happened for a reason. She was grateful for being watched over by an angel, and I for being the angel's voice.

****

Personal guides are those spirits whom we have known and loved but have departed before us. They are very much alive and well, and frankly quite busy progressing. I know, because my Pa and others tell me all about it. Our personal guides come to us when we think of them. So many of my clients have been told, "We are only a thought away," and they truly are. Personal guides come when we are in need, whether we want the advice or not. They'll try to influence us in a dream perhaps, to help us a make a wiser decision. For you see, it's not that they are all knowing since they left the physical world, it is just that they have peripheral vision. They can see all sides to a situation and therefore can help you far better than they could have while in body. Many of my clients have received a specific sign from a loved one; a nod, a tap, a tickle, so they are able to communicate and receive confirmation from a loved one.

Countless clients have released tremendous grief when they were comforted with the knowledge that their loved ones were and are truly alive and still with them.

One client stands out quite vividly. A mother had lost her six-year-old son in a car accident. Unless you have gone through this type of loss, you can't imagine the grief that takes hold; sometimes it lasts a lifetime. That's what the pain was like for her. She came to me to stop smoking. While in trance, her son came to her and told her, "Stop crying for me, Mommy. I'm fine. I'm playing with lots of other boys and girls and learning a lot in my new school. I see you and Daddy crying all the time and it makes me so sad. I want to tell you that you don't have to cry anymore because I'm not hurt. I'm with Grandma and Grandpa and they say, "Be happy for my brother, Markie." He needs you now, but you keep crying for me. I play with him a lot. He sees me. I wish you could. Then you would know that I'm all right. He wants you to play with him too, but you hurt too much. This hurts him too. Mommy, please try hard to quit smoking. The smoke hurts Markie, and he needs you to be with him for a long time. He's worried about you and Daddy. He thinks you are going to leave him, too. I told him you weren't, but he's scared. Don't worry about me, Mommy. I'm happy and I'll keep coming to visit all of you. I love you, and hugs and kisses to Daddy."

The mother felt goose bumps up and down her spine and then felt a whisper of a kiss on her cheek. This made her shiver and cry. I started to cry, too. We cried in each other's arms for a while, because we knew that what we experienced was real. We were both elated and profoundly touched by the genuine concern and wisdom of her little loving personal guide.

****

There are guides for everything under the sun, career, health, motivation, spiritual growth, artistic talent, and so on. We are assigned specific guides to assist us in our life's journey but come across many others who are attracted to us at different stages in our development. For example, Eagle Feather is a Native American spirit guide who has been assigned to me since birth. It is his job to make sure I stay on my divine plan, my healing path. Dr. Lee is a spirit physician who visits when I am ill. Dr. Shapiro comes when I need inspiration. Sister Beatrice comes only when I do work with laying on of hands, and Dora visits when I need to be more playful. I'm sure there are many, many other guides in a room when I'm working intensely with clients – both mine and theirs. Sometimes I see their forms in my client's aura; many times, the client sees them while in hypnosis; sometimes they see them in a waking state immediately following a session. It's always a surprise to them and myself when they say something like, "He's standing right next to you."

I have not been able to see a physical manifestation as clearly as my clients do, but I can always feel their presence. Sometimes I'll feel a chill up my spine or down my arm, sometimes a strum like a harp through my body, and sometimes a warm cozy feeling around my heart. Almost always I get goose bumps. This I feel is an easy sign for most people to experience. Probably most everyone has felt them, but never really thought about it.

I converse with specific guides when I need guidance. My mood will usually dictate how I will communicate. If I had a peaceful day, I would ask a question and receive a response with a head nod forward for yes, or side to side for no. If I am feeling stressed, I will eagerly go into meditation and ask to receive guidance through feelings, words, or sensations. Meditation always rejuvenates me and makes me feel much better. I usually hold an amethyst crystal in my hand to help my mind clear and clarify. Sometimes, I feel an urge to write, so I will grab my journal, ask a question in my mind, and just let my hand write. And then, of course, there is the dream. Assistance from our teachers can come to us easily if we are open to receiving them. It is important to state that they will guide and advise but will never tell us what to do It is up to us to make our own decisions and take action, because God gave us free will. Guides cannot and will not order or command us to do anything. We, not them, are responsible for our own thoughts and actions. They are shining stars that help us find our way in the thick forest of life.

On the top of the hierarchy are the great Masters. These spirit beings are the purest and wisest, and they penetrate the most profound love and light to all humanity and God's creatures. I believe Jesus, Mary, Moses, Buddha, Mohammed, and any other child of God who has earned their right to be there, fits into this arena. This is only my belief, but I believe we are all God's children striving to be as pure of light as the masters. Our school is earth, and the process, reincarnation. The goal, then, is to be as Christ-like, Buddha-like, Moses-like, or Mohammed-like as possible. To live and be as pure of heart as they are. That is the reason for the soul's continual development. We are all on the same journey toward perfection, pure light. In a way it is like our educational system; some of us reincarnate at second grade, while others jump right in at college level. Each lifetime teaches us lessons that hopefully accelerate our development to the next grade or level. It doesn't matter how long it takes to get there, but rather that we do.

So, the Masters, I suppose, are like some caring, humane CEOs in major corporations. Their job is to oversee and make sure light, love and natural order is working according to the Divine Plan. A level or two below them may be senior guides or vice presidents who delegate assignments to our teaching and personal guides. Level upon level of purity and spiritual expertise; just like the corporate ladder. We attract spirit guides who are vibrating at the same level we are on and higher. These teachers and personal guides eagerly assist us in our individual purpose. By helping us, they help themselves. It is a continual process of give and take for everyone.

Some of you may not agree with this philosophy. It's okay, because our experience is what matters. It's like a bicycle wheel. The rim holds many different spokes – all leading to the center or core of its origin. It doesn't matter which spoke one travels on to get to the core of God, what matter is that one gets there!

CHAPTER NINE

EXTRATERRESTRIALS

*S*tatistics show that over eighty percent of Americans believe in angels, and approximately the same number of people believe that there are other life forms in our universe. So, when I was first introduced to an extraterrestrial, I wasn't the least bit afraid nor surprised. Frankly, I was always wondering when one or two would show up through a client. Finally, in late September of 1994, one did – by the name of Laxzarus.

I was working in hypnosis with Marilyn, a fellow hypnotherapist, when Laxzarus introduced himself. He came about so unexpectedly; just announcing that he wanted to speak. He spoke through Marilyn and said, "I am here to serve you. This is not your imagination but the words of another being from another star system, known to you as Sirius. I have chosen Marilyn because her vibration is best suited and complimentary to mine. You may refer to me as Laxzarus.

DT: Why have you come today?

Laxzarus: I am here to assist in this work that Marilyn agreed to do.

DT: What kind of work are you talking about?

Laxzarus: We are working with vibrational patterns of light and sound to assist in the transmutation of energy for the earth's inhabitants. This is part of a much greater orchestration directed now at earth from various systems. I am specifically working with the entity known as Marilyn.

DT: What exactly is Marilyn's role in this work?

Laxzarus: She had done this before in prior existences. She knows how to heal with this method. It will all become very clear. It will become clear once she begins to work with the energies. Yes, Marilyn will work on experimentation for she has accepted this mission, prior to her birth in this incarnation. She will learn the techniques by feeling it. She's kinesthetic; her touch is very electrical and magnetic. It is one of her many gifts.

DT: What is expected of her? Where does she begin?

Laxzarus: England. She needs to gather existing information from the Institute of Color and Light, and the Institute of Sound and Toning. Reference work is already formulated throughout your world in sound, tone, and vibration. Many musicians are involved. This will be the preliminary base, buy Marilyn's research will be especially unique in its nature. What will come from her work is different; it goes beyond what already exists. It is for the next millennium more so than for the time that we are currently transmitting to. Do you understand?

DT: I think so. But can you please be more specific as to how all this work will take place?

Laxzarus: She will be guided with channeled information; specifically oriented with the light vibration's effect on the patient or person being healed. Where then the graduation or shifts in color tone occur. Must emphasize tone. Marilyn must develop inner sense of proper tone of color. Do you understand?

DT: I'm not sure. Please continue.

Laxzarus: Color has tone.

DT: Wait, I see the color purple all over now. It's changing to lavender, now blue, now back to purple. It's the tone of color; meaning it's depth and shade.

Laxzarus: Yes, but more. It is much deeper. It resonates with sound. These must be combined.

DT: How? How can she further her development to understand and incorporate these principals of color and sound healing?

Laxzarus: It will be developed as she works, but again I state that she has done this before. Marilyn will create balance by matching perfect pitch with perfect color. If perfect match has not occurred, then the application will be worthless. Also, there is another element. Each individual has his or her own tone. You must integrate that tone with the perfect match from the color and sound in order to harmonize the energies at play. Then healing will result. This will be developed through her faculties.

DT: This technique sounds very intricate and involved. Does she understand how to apply the sound and color in order to create this matching balance that you speak of?

Laxzarus: She will be guided and receive inspiration through her second sight, auditory, and kinesthetic channels as we mentioned earlier. Must emphasize electromagnetic influence, where energy is dispersed and focused. This exchange occurs on the inner planes. You do not need to concern yourselves about this. However, she must first find the imbalance of energy here in the electromagnetic field. Do you understand?

DT: Yes, I believe I do. In other words, Marilyn will receive channeled information through her primary senses; psychically, auditorily, and kinesthetically. She will first receive signals as to an

75

imbalance or disturbance in the electromagnetic field of a patient. Then she will experiment with colored light and sound to create a perfect blend of both in order to harmonize with the patient's own "tone." Is this correct?

Laxzarus: Yes, but the actual application is much more in depth. While in trance, Marilyn will be guided as to which colors and sound to blend, along with other energies that you or she is not aware of. These energies deal with magnetic energy. We are here to assist in proper magnetization with the body and its energy systems. There is a magnetic aspect that must be considered, not just electrical in nature. Do you understand?

DT: Oh! Something is forming in my hands. It's like a ball with energy. I can feel its pull. It's like a manipulation of energy. Is this correct?

Laxzarus: Yes, however, it requires focus. Energy or what you call "light" is guided into the hands of the experimenter. The effect of this light is very much occurring on a molecular level. This is causing the dispersion of energy at the same time. Energy must be reorganized by the magnetic properties and not be allowed to completely disperse. Do you follow me here?

DT: Oh boy...this is getting pretty heavy. I guess you're talking about technique in the electromagnetic field. Right?

Laxzarus: Don't worry. Marilyn will be guided, as we have said. She will meet and work with experts in these areas of color, light, and sound. They have the mathematics and science to correctly interpret the research and categorize the results. It must be scientifically oriented, not quasi-science. For your medical establishment will not accept otherwise, and the work to follow must be recognized and used if true balance of the systems is to occur. All that we have spoken of will be guided in correct time. We will assist in the precipitation of those thought forms that will manifest the flow of those events that she requires for the work that lies ahead. Trust.

DT: This is pretty amazing. I hope Marilyn is ready for it. One more question. Why are you doing this for us? What I mean is, why Earth?

Laxzarus: There are many of us who come to assist in this great time of change for your planet. There is great imbalance caused by great injustice, and on all levels. Earth is in need of cleansing, and that is why we have come at this time. As in your words, "You need all the help you can get."

I thanked Laxzarus for coming, before I brought Marilyn back up to full beta consciousness. My head was spinning. There was so much that transpired, and I hoped to God that the recorder was working, because there was no way that I was going to remember it all. I knew that she didn't have a clue, because she was too deep to have any conscious recollection of Laxzarus, let alone his intense message through her own lips.

DT: Marilyn, do you remember anything?

Marilyn: No. All I felt was a deep sense of peace, and yet a powerful energy surged through me. I could really feel it. It was weird. Not frightening, but very powerful, nonetheless. A very masculine feeling. So, what happened? What are these feelings all about?

DT: Wait till you hear. You're going to love it, I hope...
You've got an incredible load of work ahead of you. And the responsibility...Oh boy...I hope you're up to it.

I could not wait to discuss what transpired. I really didn't understand much about what Laxzarus was talking about, but as we conversed, it became apparent that she understood quite easily.

He was right: she did do this before, but in previous lifetimes. This explained why the information was not as difficult for her as it was for me. I wished her success in her future endeavor, and secretly was glad it was her destiny and not mine. That's a lot on one person's plate, but then again, Laxzarus said she agreed to it. Again, I was reminded of the prebirth blueprint; a plan that outlines our goals and direction – an agenda we agree upon prior to birth. I was comfortable with the fact that this was indeed part of Marilyn's divine plan. I was glad that I had the opportunity to share in her experience. I also had to admit that I was thrilled to talk with anther life form from another galaxy. I always believed that they existed, but until you communicate and feel their distinctive presence, maybe only then can you comfortably state, "I know extraterrestrials exist." I was fortunate to have an experience with a friendly one. I'm sure that, as on our planet, there are ETs who are not so nice. I was thankful that my first introduction was pleasant. I've heard all about abductions, and destructive alien forces that are better left outside my door. I suppose if God wanted me to learn from that negativity, he would create that experience for me. All I can say is, "Thank you God, for not doing it."

****

My second exposure to other life forms didn't occur again until 1996. A client named Lisa sought understanding to a lifelong depression and a strange habit. She explained that her depression did not stem from early childhood or an unhappy personal adult life. She loved her husband, kids and career. She was quite active in her community and loved the way life turned out for her. However, behind the outward appearance lay a tremendous grief for earth and all its inhabitants. Every time she allowed herself to appreciate nature, animals or acts of kindness from strangers, she would break into an uncontrollable bout of crying which ended in despair. She couldn't help herself. It was automatic. Even as a young child she would mourn for Mother Earth's inevitable loss of life. Her parents were upset with her "wild imagination of gloom and doom" and couldn't handle their child's remorse. So, Lisa was told to ignore her feelings in order to live peacefully in the family. She did but cried secretly in her bed night after night. She learned to hide her feelings well, but unfortunately it manifested itself in the form of a very strange habit. She couldn't sit! When it was required to do so, she did, of course, but with great anxiety. It was actually quite uncomfortable for her to do so. Not physically, but emotionally and spiritually. She felt much more compelled to stand all the time. It wasn't out of fear, but rather out of comfort. Standing was a natural posture for her. Sitting, on the other hand, was like crawling. We all can crawl, of course, but for how long? It just doesn't feel natural or comfortable for us to do so. That's how sitting felt to Lisa: unnatural. Standing was the preferred and automatic position of choice. She eventually found a way to live and adjust to her requirements, and I admired her for her courage and ingenuity. However, I couldn't wait to see why this need to stand – for it truly was a need to stand, rather than an aversion to sit – became manifested.

DT: Lisa, I don't know if you're going to find all your answers. I do know however, that you will receive exactly what your higher self wants you to. Whatever comes will be for your highest good, so if you're ready, let's begin.

(After the induction, Lisa slid easily into a medium level trance.)

Lisa: (She broke out into a cold sweat, breathing heavily, and started to cry. The tears become more hurried, while the moaning increased.) It's so sad, so sad...I can't stay here because it's killing me.

DT: Lisa, you don't have to feel all the emotions. You can rise above and observe it if you wish. What do you say?

Lisa: No, I can't ignore the feelings. I've always ignored the feelings, but they just keep getting stronger and stronger. The pain in my heart is so deep. I can't stop crying. I can't control it. (I honored her necessity to release the pain through crying, and waited until she calmed down a little so we could continue with our conversation. After a few more minutes, I realized that she was not going to calm herself without help, so I told her to go to her favorite place: a place where she felt safe, warm, and loved. Lisa stopped crying and began taking slow deep breaths to relax herself even more.)

DT: I guess you are there...your favorite spot where you feel warm, safe, and loved.

Lisa: Hmmm.

DT: Tell me about it. What's it like?

Lisa: I'm home.

DT: The house where you live now or the one you grew up in?

Lisa: No, home. (She grinned a beautiful smile, and her whole demeanor changed to one of peace and serenity.)

DT: I don't understand. Which home are you talking about?

Lisa: I'm not on earth, nor in body. Just vibration. I can hear you, feel you, see you, and know your thoughts and feelings, but I don't need the physical plane of existence in the same way you do.

DT: I'm not sure I understand. Have you left the body? Are you in an in-between state, in the light?

Lisa: No. I am home. This is where I truly belong. It is hard for me to explain to you because there are no words in your language that would accurately describe my existence. However, I will work with what you have in order to make clear my purpose. My home is in another galaxy; many, many star systems away. What you would call light years away. We do not need a physical body.

We live on vibrational energy. The sound of my home is like your heartbeat. There is a continual soothing beat that vibrates amongst us all. We do not need food, water, or shelter to survive. However, we do need love and a sense of purpose. We are highly mental energies and are in need of procreating our emotional and spiritual vibrations for growth. Your species has much emotional opportunities. We are attracted to you because of the growth your planet provides us.

DT: So, you are an extraterrestrial visiting our planet through Lisa?

Lisa: Not exactly. Yes, I am an extraterrestrial to you, but I am not visiting. I chose the vehicle to be born into prior to Lisa's birth. Lisa and I are one and the same. I did not come to visit and share her body, but rather to be incarnated as a human for this growth experience.

DT: You're kidding! You mean extraterrestrials can be born as human beings? Does the human being know they might be from another planet? I mean, are they somehow aware of this fact? And if they are, do they possess the same powers as you do? (The questions were pouring out of my mouth one right after the other. I was so shocked and thrilled at the fact that there were more beings to our earthly existences than just human ones. I was a little kid in a candy story again. Thinking about the soul being an intergalactic traveler was exhilarating for me. It was something I had never thought about before, and for the first time I wondered if I was an extraterrestrial too!)

Lisa: So many questions; I will try to answer as best I can. Yes, it is an absolute fact that many from my home planet, as well as others from other galaxies, have chosen to be born into human bodies at this precise time in your history. It has been done since the birth of your planet Earth, but many more have chosen this time to be of service. As to the question of awareness, most ET/

human beings are not consciously aware but rather very much so in the subconscious domain. If it were obvious to the conscious mind, then what true growth would occur? Our choice to incarnate (not reincarnate for this is not our home planet) is twofold: First, we have come to further our emotional and spiritual growth by learning how to feel our negative emotions and then transform them into spiritual enlightenment. And second, we have come to serve this planet by offering our expertise in technology, healing modalities, and physical cleansing of the environment. There is much suffering from disease, disorder and decay. Both individually and planetarily. We hear the cries that literally strike a discord in our peaceful vibration. To not listen and ignore would create a disharmony in our world. As you can see, it benefits us all to help. For by helping you, we help ourselves as well.

DT: Why is it so important for you to come now? Earth has always had destructive forces in her history.

Lisa: Many from all over the galaxy and galaxies beyond have heard Earth's cries and have come to help in any way they can. Earth has always had her problems, yes, that is true. But she has never been abused to the point of destruction, as she is in the present. It would be similar in thought to a young adolescent male who recklessly abuses his mind and body, not thinking of the negative consequences that will undoubtedly occur a few years down the road. For example, a young man chooses to disobey all the laws that govern his existence: parental, governmental, bodily, educational, spiritual laws, and so on. He begins his fall by ignoring his parents' rules and dishonors them by speaking painfully rude to them. He chooses to disobey society's laws by doing drugs and robbing other people to pay for his destructive habit. His body laws are broken because he has chosen to poison his body with drugs, alcohol, and other dead foods that will cause havoc in his physical system. In addition, his mental capabilities will decline because of all the poisons that have entered into his brain. His desire to learn will be destroyed because of an apathetic attitude, and his spirit will wither, due to lack of love and self-esteem. Only negative thought will enter his mind, because that is what he is thinking and feeling. Sadly, negative action will follow. With all this mental, emotional, physical, and spiritual decay, the young adult is surely on a downhill course. An early death could evolve, but more likely he will waste his precious young life drifting endlessly unaware of his life's purpose.

This boy is in desperate need of immediate change: First, recognition of the negative state in which he has forsaken to. Second, a cleansing of the poisons from all aspects of self is vital, in order to create perfect balance, and third, a reawakening to his true self...a transformation in order to fulfill his life's mission. For we all have a mission; a purpose to why we are here. And that is why we are here...to help in the recognition, cleansing and transformation of your planet. Like the young adult, Earth's inhabitants have made poor choices as well. We are here to help.

DT: What is your specific role then? What have you come to do?

Lisa: (As soon as I asked that, Lisa started to breathe quickly, and the tears started to roll down her cheeks. She paused for quite some time, and then the sobbing began again.) I'm so sad, so sad. I can't speak because the tears are blocking my throat. It hurts so bad to feel this way.

DT: Lisa, try to speak. It is important that we find out what exactly makes you so sad. On the count of three you'll be able to tell me exactly what's troubling you. One...two...three...

Lisa: I cry for Earth. I see her drying up and dying. I feel her agony of despair, as her waters and environment become destroyed with pollutants, and I hear her vibrational cries. They are a groan of deep remorse and grief. Unbearable.

DT: (The sobbing became so intense at this point that I really didn't know what to do or say. In my perplexed moment a distinct voice inside my head told me what to ask.) Are all these emotions that you are experiencing from different senses part of your development? What I mean is, does this profound compassion stem from a human prophecy of doom, or is it part of your divine plan for emotional and spiritual growth?

Lisa: (As suddenly as she started crying, she stopped. She paused for a minute and then spoke. It was obvious that she had come to a realization.) Yes, it is part of the plan. I'm learning to feel what it's like to be human. Yet, I continue to feel the same way that I'm accustomed to...sensing everything around me in it's true state of being. When I say I see, feel, and hear Earth – I actually do. This is not a figure of speech, but rather an actuality. I've been feeling, but in my own familiar way, and obviously to the extreme. More is not better. I thought it was for my own emotional and spiritual growth, but unfortunately, I haven't accomplished my purpose. I have been in pain because of my own empathetic abilities. I've been feeling everyone else's pain except my own. I thought it was my own, but how incorrect I was. I was feeling the collective consciousness of Earth and all its inhabitants. Foolish me. (She started to cry again, but this time it was soft and gentle.)

DT: Whose tears do these belong to, you or Earth?

Lisa: (A smile appeared on her face.) Mine.

DT: How wonderful that you are learning to feel like a real human being! Congratulations!

Lisa: (Her tears broke out into a giggle.) Yes, it's quite odd to feel happy while you're crying. It is quite wonderful, isn't it?

DT: Yes, it is. I do it all the time. I've got one more question for you though. Why is it that you prefer to stand rather than sit?

Lisa: Oh that...I'm not used to having the confinement of

being in a physical body. It's much more comfortable for me to be vertical, that's all.

DT: Were you aware of any of this before today?

Lisa: No. Well, maybe. I had dreams. Lots of them when I was younger. I would fly out of my body to a place where I felt warm, safe, and loved.

DT: Well, we know where that is, don't we?

Lisa: Yes, it's home.

DT: Yes, like Dorothy said, "There's no place like home." (She opened up her eyes and smiled at me. It was clear that she brought herself out of hypnosis.)

We both laughed and stared at each other to ponder this incredible experience. She hugged me, thanked me, and left. I can never thank her enough for the awakening that she gave me.

CHAPTER TEN

ENTITY ATTACHMENT AND RELEASE

*J*ust the thought of The Exorcist sends chills up and down my spine. I remember sitting in a Manhattan movie theater gripping the side of the seat out of sheer fear. Even though I was raised Jewish, a part of me believed in the devil. I was a kid and got the creeps like everyone else. However, my non-Jewish friends were twice as scared as me! To console our fears, we convinced ourselves that it's just not possible for a real-life possession. After all, we were all sane and living in the twentieth century. Those type of events are pure fantasy made up in Hollywood. Little did I know that those events really can and do occur, and not necessarily in an evil, harmful sense.

As a hypnotherapist, I have been introduced to all kinds of attachments. "Attachments" is a better word to define the circumstance (real-life possession) since the entity or spirit of a deceased person attaches themselves to a living person. This entity can influence, help, hinder, or hurt a person, but I don't believe they possess a person, due to the soul's fee will give by God. I could be wrong. Maybe they can, but in my practice, I have not witnessed or experienced a true possession as seen in The Exorcist. Honestly, I hope I never do!

In any case, entities attach for very specific reasons: some are lost and can't find the light; some may know exactly where the light is, but are afraid to go to the light out of fear of retribution; others may attach because they don't know they are dead; others may be deceased loved ones with unfinished business, or are stuck in an earthbound state due to grieving living relatives; some may be past-life entities with karmic ties who can't let go; and some may be dark, evil entities who purposely play havoc in a body. They are the souls who have been very negative in their life or lifetimes and refuse to go to the light; while other dark ones, who never had a body, are thought forms created by the dark forces to procreate more and more negativity through conversion during attachment. And then there are attachments by living souls who are obsessed with another living person. There are probably more circumstances, but the ones just mentioned I have personally encountered with clients.

The "lost ones" are the most common and easiest to recognize. They come right out and tell you who they are and why they attached in the first place. Usually, they do not have an emotional bond with the person but attached to them because it was easy to do so. Let me explain. Entities can travel freely through the astral plane and into our physical plane. They are without a body, so it is easy for them to enter into one if a living person's aura or magnetic field is weak or has a hole or tear in it. Do not confuse an entity with a highly evolved ET. The ET who didn't have a body, as in Lisa's case, was highly evolved and didn't need one to exist. An entity, in most cases, was a human being who had lost its body at death.

In the few instances when a possessing entity declares it never had a body, the only assumption that can be made is that the entity was never human but rather a low vibrating life-form (created by thoughts) whose main purpose is to create havoc and disharmony in the human being it has attached to. You can tell the difference between a low-level nonhuman entity, and a highly evolved ET how you feel in its presence. If you feel uncomfortable and uneasy, then your instinct will lead you to a correct evaluation of a negative or low-level entity. If you feel comfortable, light, and energized, then you can assume that the energy present is one of a high vibration. Think of the human body as a spiral of energy that continually spins and vibrates. When the mind, body, and spirit are strong, then the spiral spins at a very fast frequency or speed. It is vibrant and in perfect health.

In contrast, when the mind or spirit become overburdened, exhausted, depressed, angered and/or resentful for an extended period of time, then the spiral slows down, which causes the body to vibrate at a much slower speed. This negative state of mind will directly affect the physical body by first forming a "dis-ease" or imbalance in the aura: a sort of physical blueprint as to what will manifest if the original negative attitude isn't recognized, understood, and then changed. It is in this blueprint stage that the wandering entity can attach itself quite easily because the body is vibrating a much slower rate.

Unfortunately, the aura has become vulnerable and can be easily penetrated. For example: Imagine you are riding on one of those amusement rides that speeds around a circular track. It's going extremely fast, and you are thrilled, elated, and full of energy. It would be impossible for someone to hop in your car because you are traveling way too fast. However, when the ride slows down, the "lost one" could hop right in and sit next to you, whether you wanted them to or not. It is the same with our bodies and entities. Most of the time we are unaware of their presence. We don't hear voices or communicate with them on a conscious level. However, they do influence us on a subconscious level. Not all, but many have a direct line to our thoughts. The "lost ones" are souls who have found a home in us. Most know they have died but are unaware that there is a light that will guide them to their true home, or they are afraid of the light because they don't believe they are dead.

When I was hypnotized by a colleague, a "Michael" came through and said that he was lost. When the hypnotherapist asked why he attached to me, he said I was close by, and it was easy to do so. Apparently, he died in the same hospital I was in when I was having my tonsils removed at age sixteen. At that time, I was miserably depressed because my boyfriend broke up with me, and I was having a surgery that I knew would be painful. This "Michael" was approximately the same age as I when he died in a car accident. I seemed like a safe and good choice, so he slid right in. When asked if he knew about the light, he did indeed, but chose to ignore it because he thought staying with me was better than admitting that he was dead. The hypnotherapist persuaded him to go to the light by telling him all about the love and opportunity that awaited him. She painted a picture that he just couldn't resist; so, Michael left as easily as he came in. I was aware of the whole conversation and amazed that he was with me for over twenty years without a clue of his existence.

****

Deceased loved ones can also make their presence known when they have something they want to say. Tony and Danielle were adult siblings who had lost their mom to cancer. They were adjusting fine on the outside, but they still had an emotional need to be in touch with their mom. Normally I do not hypnotize two people at the same time in such a personal session, but they both had the same need to somehow communicate with Mom. So, I hypnotized them together. They both relaxed into hypnosis quite easily. Tony was an auditory and visual subject, meaning he could easily see and hear an experience, whereas Danielle was more kinesthetic and visual; she felt and saw an experience as it was happening. Once the two were in a suitably deep trance, I had them both select a photograph in their mind of themselves with their mom somewhere between the ages of ten and fifteen. They both happily described their photograph and detailed the scenes that took place. They were then asked to jump into the photograph and be a part of that scene once again. Reliving the experience was wonderful; especially when they felt the presence of their mom.

At that moment, Mom spoke up through Tony. What was interesting is the fact that Danielle was able to witness her mom speaking. Mom described how she hung around all three of her children to help them adjust to her death and help them in their daily lives. She knew about the light, in fact was visited by many of her relatives to come join them in the light but refused to go. She insisted on staying because the third child, Angela, was having a terrible time coping; she was making wrong choices in her life and needed Mom around to straighten her out. Every time Tony and Danielle would say, "Mom, go' to the light. We'll take care of Angela, don't worry. We will watch out for her," Mom would just get annoyed and yell at the two kids to stop telling her what to do. This amused Tony and Danielle because they stated, "Mom hasn't changed one bit!"

I attempted to persuade Mom to go with her relatives; I called everyone in – her parents, brother, etc., but she told them they can visit her all they like but she won't go with them until she can talk to Angela. Needless to say, Tony and Danielle were thrilled that Mom was "alive" and hadn't changed, but disturbed that she refused to continue her growth in the light. They weren't upset that she attached herself to them, traveling between siblings at her will; after all it was Mom. They were upset by her stubbornness and adamant refusal to go to the light. Mom had unfinished business, and it was as simple as that.

****

My first meeting with a "dark one" was an eyeopener to say the least. I had worked with Marsha for over two years and felt I knew her well. She initially came to see me because of a chronic disability that prevented her from doing what she wanted to do. The disability was not permanent but rather limited her range of motion in her neck and back. She sought me out because she honestly thought that there might be something else behind the physical problem. In the early sessions we uncovered past lives, and incidents in the early childhood of the present life that contributed to the problem, but it never seemed to provide the complete answer. Like an onion, she needed to be peeled layer by layer in order for her higher self to allow subconscious material to filter into her conscious mind. I truly believe God doesn't give you anything you can't handle, and I guess he thought Marsha was ready at the next session.

DT: Go where you need to go, where that may be for your highest good.

Marsha: I'm trapped in a wire meshed cage and can't get out. (She appeared to be quite disturbed and a little frightened. Her breathing became rushed, as she waited to respond. It was difficult at first to get a response from her, for she hesitated on her first words. I knew that it was going to be a challenge to work with her in this particular session.)

DT: How did you find yourself in this entanglement? What does it mean? (Still no answer). Does it represent a physical entanglement, an emotional or spiritual one? (Still no answer.) A past life?

Marsha: No, other spirits.

DT: What do you mean? (I knew what she meant, and my worst fears were about to come true. I could tell by the way she was acting that whoever came to visit wasn't someone from the light. It gave me the creeps, literally, because the energy in the room changed to a sticky, heavy weight. It was dark energy, and I knew it. My left arm felt the density of the negative energy, and it scared me. Part of me wanted to stop the session before I got in too deep. What if I didn't know what to do? What if I got really, really scared? Maybe I couldn't help her...but how could I abandon her now when she needed me most?) How are these spirits affecting you?

Marsha: In a negative way. (Chills went up my spine. I started to breathe just as shortly and quickly as she.)

DT: How many entities are there?

Marsha: Four.

DT: Is there a leader among them?

Marsha: Yes.

DT: Well, let me speak to anyone who is homesick...to experience love and light. Who wants to go home to the light? How many would love to see loved ones in the light? (I had to change gears first, because I started to hyperventilate and knew I wasn't ready to conquer the leader just yet.)

Marsh: Two.

DT: Come forward now. Who speaks first?

Marsha: Paula. (Just then, her whole mannerism and body position changed. She softened and became quite relaxed.)

DT: Paula, I'd like to talk to you directly. We need to know why you attached to Marsha?

Paula: I need to grow.

DT: How old were you when you attached to Marsha, and how old was she?

Paula: We were both four.

DT: Are you still four years old?

Paula: Yes, that's why I need to grow. I thought I would grow with her but I didn't She did, but I didn't. (She is crying now.)

DT: Why are you so sad?

Paula: Because I'm lost. I lost my mommy and can't find her.

DT: Would you like to go to a place where you feel warm and safe? A place where you feel love all around you?

Paula: Maybe. But I want to find my mommy first.

DT: Well, let's see who comes to visit us. Maybe that special someone can help us find your mommy. On the count from one to three, anyone who loves and cares about Paula, come forth now. One...two...three.

Paula: Mommy! Mommy! I found you! (Before I could even suggest that she go to the light with her mom, they were off in a flash.)

(Boy that was easy. It actually felt good to reunite a mother and daughter. I was feeling lighter and better now, more confident. May it wasn't a dark force after all. I was probably allowing my imagination to get the best of me. How silly of me. I should know better!)

DT: How many entities are still attached to Marsha?

Marsha: Three.

DT: I know you just witnessed a beautiful reunion for Paula. Who else wants to feel just as happy and loved as she? Come forward, I know you are there. (I saw a shift in Marsha's expression and body language, so I waited.) What's your name?

Marsha: John.

DT: How long has it been since you've seen your loved ones? (No answer.) Do you want to go back home?

John: No.

DT: Why not? What are you so afraid of? On the count of three you'll tell me, one...two...three... (Still no response.) Why did you attach to Marsha?

John: It's easy to attach to her.

DT: What makes Marsh so easy?

John: She opens to us.

DT: When does she allow herself to open to you? (No response.)

Why did you choose to stay with her rather than go to the light? Do you want me to help you? You know I can. What do you want most of all? (Still no response.) How old are you?

John: Nine.

DT: Don't you miss Mommy and Daddy?

John: No.

DT: Oh...well, wouldn't you rather be in a place where you can rum, jump and play? A place where there is love?

John: There is no love.

DT: Well, the smartest boys know that the place that has lots of love in it is a place where they can have fun. They can build, paint, explore, and do about anything they want to do. And they always feel proud of themselves. Wouldn't you like to feel proud of yourself?

John: Yes.

DT: Anyone who cares and loves John, please show yourself to him now. John open yourself up to the light. Do you see the light?

John: Yes.

DT: Allow yourself to be warmed and loved by the light. Let the light fill you up completely. On the count of three, you'll be able to see who travels in the light to see you, one...two...three... Who do you see?

John: Nana. She's smiling at me and says I should go with her. I want to go with her.

DT: Say goodbye to Marsha and thank her.

John: Thank you.

DT: Now go to the land of love with Nana. (At this moment, I actually felt a slight, swift zap of energy through my body. It felt electrical and tingly. It was as if they left Marsha, took a detour through me, and then went on their way.) Marsha, do you feel any different now that Paula and John left? (Just then I watched in horror as her face and body contorted into an ugly expression. My fear was back, and in full force! I knew I couldn't handle it alone, my anxiety was swelling by the second, so I called out loud for angelic intervention.) Archangel Michael, Raphael, the healer and protector, come forth now in my time of need. (I assumed that they would be there for me because I asked. My belief in this assumption gave me the courage to continue.) On the count of three, whoever remains with Marsha, come forward now, one...two...three... Speak your name. (Silence.) Do you want to be helped?

Marsha: (She grunted as she shook her head slowly to say no.)

DT: Don't you want to feel wonderful, joy and peace?

Marsha: (Again, another grunt as she hissed back to me.) No.

DT: Who are you? What is your name? Why have you attached yourself to Marsha? What is it? You don't want to talk? Are you from the light? (I obviously knew the answer, but because I was so nervous I rambled on with questions. Besides, the entity wasn't responding anyway so I continued on.) Are you afraid of the light? You cannot lie in the presence of Michael and Raphael. Are you from the dark side?

Marsha: Yes.

DT: (I thought that the chills that ran up my spine would freeze me to death! I don't know how I continued, but I did.) Make a choice to go to the light now, if you have the courage. Michael and Raphael are here to help you. Choose to go to the light with them... all will be forgiven. The light is more powerful than the dark. It offers freedom and forgiveness. (Marsha is now thrashing back and forth in the chair, in obvious distress.) Do you want to be forgiven? Come on now. You can't be as bad as you think you are. What could you have done that would make you think that you are unforgivable?

Marsha: I killed all the children. (She laughed as she said it, and then slowly grinned a sinister smile.)

DT: (At that moment I thought I would die. All I could think of was The Exorcist movie and how the priest was thrown out the window! My anxiety level reached to point of severe alarm. My heart was pounding as it never did before. The sweat poured off my body and stained my clothes. The more I panicked, the more she laughed. I felt helpless in a power play, and knew my fear was the killer's lifeblood. I wanted to scream, run away, and forget the fact that my son was sound asleep in the next room. I was stuck in a gripping terror and couldn't help myself. I knew I had to overcome this destructive mental war, but I was powerless. I succumbed to my own weakness, but not before I spoke to God.) Lord, you know how I'm feeling. I need you now more than ever before. I don't know what to do. Please guide me and show me the way. Please Lord, please don't abandon me... (Just then I remembered the angels I had called in earlier to assist me. I called out to them.) Michael, Raphael, if you're really here, send in your army and trap this dark entity. Send him to the light. I need you and need you now. Help me!

Marsha: (She laughed harder and louder. The shrill sound of her voice made me shake. I felt so defeated. The angels weren't with me after all. My belief system was baloney, and I was devastated along with being terrorized. I started to feel numb. Just then she spoke but it was not her own voice.) You're such an idiot. What makes you think your angels are stronger than me and my dark army? They stand beside you all right, but they are useless in helping you conquer my will. You gave me a choice to stay or leave with them. I choose to stay and torture Marsha, and others like her. She is a fool spending money and time on doctors and people like you. She thinks it is of her own making...it is to a degree. She is easily manipulated by me and the others, and we thrive on her negativity. I have caused her great pain, and I plan to continue. You better leave now before we attach to you also. For we can, and quite easily too, because your fear gives us easy access. You are losing the battle, but you already know this don't you? Let's see what your skin feels like... (It laughed and laughed.)

DT: (At this point, I humbly prayed to God once again, but this time without fear. I already yielded to the fear, but not to "It". No matter what this dark entity said, he wasn't going to take away my love and faith in God, even if he entered me. I had to keep believing that it was all happening for a reason. I had to trust in God. It was all I had left. Just then Marsha spoke up.)

Marsha: He's gone.

DT: What do you mean, gone? Where is he? In me?

Marsha: No. He's gone. He went to the light. Mother Mary took him.

DT: I don't understand. What happened?

Marsha: I could see, hear, and feel, and even smell him. He was ugly and horrible looking. There were others too, but not as horrible as him. He was scary. He was hanging around my neck and pinching all the discs on my spine. It was gross and painful. I could feel your fear too. The more fearful you became, the more panicked I became. I couldn't move though. I was glued in the chair and couldn't scream either. I was just as stuck as you. And I saw Michael and Raphael just like you said. They were standing next to you observing the scene. I kept trying to talk to them, but I couldn't. I kept wondering why they couldn't help us, but I couldn't reach them. Then Mary came out of nowhere and started to whisper to the Entity. I couldn't hear them, but I saw her take his hand, and then he left with her. The others followed them. (At that moment Marsha opened her eyes and looked at me with a startled look.) It's her. It's Mary.

DT: What do you mean?

Marsha: Mary. She's here. She's standing next to you. I can see her, can't you?

DT: No... but I can feel her. (I closed my eyes and said, "Mary, thank you for coming and saving us. I'm forever grateful." Tears swept down my cheeks. I knew I had experienced a powerful lesson.)

Marsha: I don't have the pain anymore. It's gone.

DT: You can thank Mary for that!

It took me quite some time to figure out exactly what that lesson was all about. God wanted me to wake up and realize that spirituality is not all rosy, fun and games. He wanted me to see the other side – the dark side. I awakened so much that day to so many different realities; the real war between light and dark, the true existence of Mary, that our own negativity and fear builds a fertile breeding ground for dark entities, and most of all – that love really does conquer all. It was love that brought the loved ones to guide Paula and John. And it was love from Mary that brought the dark one back home to God.

****

Jillian taught me about past-life ties, and living attachments – a very interesting case indeed. I knew her as an acquaintance but enjoyed her company immensely. Even though we could chat on and on, neither one of us knew the other was into metaphysics. On one occasion, I went to see her unannounced and found her to be quite distressed. She confided that she had experienced a strange phenomenon when she recently attended a rock concert. During the concert, she went into a spontaneous regression. She had found herself in a hallway with big arched windows. She felt she was somehow back in time during the medieval period in history. The hallway was filled with a white fog, but she could see someone standing at the end of the room – it was the rock star she had gone to see at the concert. She began to move through fog, floating towards him, feeling a great warmth and love. The feeling intensified as she traveled closer to him, and then suddenly she broke into hysterical sobs. Jillian came out of trance. She was dumfounded by her experience and her inability to stop crying. Why this experience happened was beyond her comprehension. She had no known affection or interest in this rock star. She was certainly not a fan of his. In fact, the only reason she had attended this concert was to join her friend who had graciously invited her. Her uncontrollable sobbing not only ruined her evening at the concert but continued almost daily for the next few months.

The dreams kept repeating themselves. They haunted her nightly. Jillian would see a big wrought-iron gate. She thought the gate symbolized a division or separation. Then she would see the rock star with two women. One was blonde and the other a redhead. One of the women would say, "It's time for us to go. You can't stay anymore."

Jillian would awaken with tremendous grief. She would cry at home, cry at work, and cry in the car. She had no idea why she was crying. All she knew was that if the dreams and crying attack didn't stop soon, she would literally have a mental breakdown. I listened to her story and then told her I was a hypnotherapist. I told her that hypnosis could be a tool to help her tap into her higher self in order to explore what was going on and hopefully offer suggestions to remedy the disturbing situation. She readily agreed because she was desperate.

The first session brought her back to a past life in Ireland. Her name was Katherine, and she lived in a small cottage in a village. She met Andrew at a dance. They were smitten at first glance and proceeded to spend much time with each other. Months passed and their love grew. However, there was turmoil and conflict all around them. Ireland was in a state of confusion and there were many battles being fought. Andrew had to leave his beloved to go fight in one of the battles. "I don't want to go," he sadly confessed, but he went anyway out of duty to his country. Katherine was heartbroken and scared at the thought of losing him. Soon, he returned, but on horseback, facing the ground. He had been shot and died in her arms. Katherine was devastated and couldn't stop sobbing. When she came back to full beta consciousness (the alert and waking state) she immediately identified Andrew as the same rock star that haunts her in her dreams.

The next session brought Jillian to England as Anna. She lived with her husband, Michael, on the coast of Cornwall. They had a baby named Randall and were quite happy living in a plain, simple cottage while working for the nobles: she as a maid, and he as a groom. Tragedy struck when Michael had gotten into an argument with a friend over money. He had been stabbed in the lower right side of his abdomen and had died instantly. Anna became hysterical, and remained depressed the rest of her life. Michael's brother took care of her and the baby, but life had no more meaning. A part of her died when Michael died. Again, Michael and the rock star were one and the same.

A third session brought Jillian to Wales as Rachael. She was a beautiful peasant girl who liked to dream lazily by a waterfall. One day her thoughts were interrupted by a handsome young man named Anthony. They flirted with one another and knew instantly that their chemistry was intensely magnetic. Secret rendezvous occurred nightly at the waterfall, because unfortunately their love was forbidden. He was wealthy and had been promised to another girl... a lady of society. Rachael was, of course, unacceptable to his world. Anthony was torn. He was madly in love with Rachael, but desperately afraid of his mother's wrath. He abruptly ended his love affair with Rachael and never saw her again. Rachael was devastated but continued on with her life, never to love or trust another man again.

After this third regression, Jillian finally understood why she was grieving. Her subconscious mind was still holding onto the memory of her interrupted love and the painful loss she experienced in three lifetimes, and with the same lover! So, the question remained: Why did her higher self-want those memories to surface and interfere with her life now?

We had trouble answering this because the dreams stopped... but spontaneous visions started! Even at work, Jillian would be attending a task when suddenly, and without warning, the rock star's face would literally appear before her very eyes. She felt stalked by an apparition which caused great anxiety, to say the least. She knew it wasn't her imagination because she could physically see him. Ironically, it didn't scare her because she didn't feel threatened by him, but rather felt an intense frustration and anger because she did not have control over the situation. This phenomenon was not only disturbing her life but brought back the grief in full force.

I began to wonder if this rock star was subconsciously haunting her for a reason. Maybe subconsciously he found his old love and wanted to be together again. Maybe he just traveled to her in her dream state to communicate with her. Maybe he was just psychically advanced enough to travel during her waking state and penetrate into her aura in order to appear to her as a spontaneous vison. Maybe a living person who obsesses over another living person can literally just attach themselves to their object of obsession. These thoughts were starting to haunt me, so I decided to share them with Jillian. She listened intently and said it made sense to her.

"I didn't ask him to come to me. In fact, I wish he never had. All he has done is cause problems in my life. I wish he would just go away."

"Why don't you tell him that?" I said. "Why don't you tell him how you feel about the way he has interrupted your life? I bet you can talk to him either in hypnosis or in meditation. In a trance state, you can communicate with him. You have nothing to lose, and everything to gain."

Jillian agreed to try. A part of her was in denial, for she couldn't see how or why a rock star could physically enter her body and attach himself to her. However, she was desperate enough and willing to try anything. So, in meditation she confronted her obsessive living entity. Jillian reported that he initially didn't respond verbally but only stared at her and walked away. She felt a remorse and grief from him too. "It was as if he was in more pain than I."

The visions ceased and her life was starting to get back to normal. Occasional dreams and bouts of crying occurred, but nothing like it had been. Then one day Jillian asked me to listen to a recording made by the rock star. I'll never forget my response, because I was driving as I was listening to the music. I had to pull over. His lyrics shot right through my soul. They spoke of his love that was centuries old; of his spirit that won't rest until he finds his love. Song after song his lyrics gave clues to the past lives that he and Jillian had experienced together. I was shocked and amazed at the confirmation, over and over again.

Jillian was still not a fan, but now a believer in spiritual realities. The experience opened up a whole new world to her. She began reading everything she could on past lives, metaphysics, and alternative healing. She attended workshops, lectures, anything that would teach her about self-love and spiritual development, purpose, and the gift of service. She was hungry for knowledge and wanted to test out what she learned, so Jillian attended a second concert. As she watched him perform, she could feel his energy all around her. He didn't torment her but rather warmed her spirit. She wondered if he could sense her vibrations too. So, she closed her eyes and quieted her mind. When her thoughts were controlled, she summoned up all the love inside of her and sent healing thoughts to him. Thoughts like, "I wish for you love and great harmony now, in this life. Heal your sadness and be not afraid for we will be together again in the afterlife. Be at peace now."

Just then the rock star stopped singing. It was as if he missed his cue or had forgotten his lyrics. He just stood there in a dazed look. At that moment Jillian felt chills run along her spine. She was certain that he felt her presence, and was thrilled that genuine thoughts of love could heal his obsession. She didn't want to meet him or start up where they had left off. They both had their own personal lives; they were both married. All she wanted and prayed for was a healing for him. That's all.

Months passed with no disturbing influences from him. Jillian was comforted in the knowledge that maybe her night at the concert got through to his soul. However, she soon realized it didn't when she stumbled upon a magazine interview of him. In it, he confided that he has a spiritual problem that no one could understand but himself. He didn't elaborate or give specifics but indicated that he was searching for an answer. Jillian got a second confirmation and wanted to somehow reach out to him. Since she realized that his attachment through obsession is destructive for both of them, she prayed to God for guidance. In meditation, she received an answer. "He may be psychically more advanced than you, but you are more spiritually developed. Everyone is on their own time frame. You can help him become spiritually awakened to his true self by praying for his highest good."

****

Jillian has done so and has progressed with her own spiritual awakening as well. When she initially asked, "Why is this happening to me?" she didn't get an answer, because she wasn't ready to receive it. Now that she has "awakened", she finally understands why. The rock star attachment was a lesson for both of them. Neither one was developing or growing in a spiritual sense. By attaching himself to her, it forced Jillian to awaken to other realities, and a purpose to her life. It forced her to wake up and move into other directions; healing areas where her primary talents can thrive.

Without this disturbing occurrence she would still be stuck in her comfortable rut and not be progressing in her joyful purpose. She realized the rock star was a catalyst for her spiritual awakening and she is forever grateful. One day she knows that he too will realize that his search is within himself, rather than for an external lost love. He will find that his own loving light has more important things to do, and when the time is right, it will find its way to her like an old flame – to be rekindled.

CHAPTER ELEVEN

UNIVERSAL LAWS

*L*ife is more than just a bowl of cherries; it's a spiritual adventure! Sometimes the going is rough, but if you're wise to the universal laws, then your sailing will be smoother than you could have ever imagined it to be.

The first universal law I learned was the ***Law of Manifestation***. This law can bring us such joy if we choose to acknowledge its existence. It's a matter of listening to our heart's desire, fueling it passionately with our imagination, and then taking action. One day I had a thought, "I want a baby!" Thoughts can be fleeting, or they can sit in your mind like a pot of soup that gets thicker and richer over time. If the thought passes quickly out of your mind, it is powerless because it has no energy to fuel it into fruition. However, if the thought is nurtured with feeling, it will travel into the subconscious mind, where it will begin to take form. Thoughts materialize in your subconscious mind first, like a blueprint ready to be built in the outside or real world. The actual building of the thought form solely depends on the passion or desire that carries the thought. Thoughts are powerful because they are alive with energy.

Not only did I think about having a baby, but I also passionately craved one. I fueled this thought with fantasies all the time, despite the fact that my conscious mind believed it was impossible. Finally, the manifestation of the thought was ready to be launched. Once the blueprint stage is complete, the actual creation or construction takes place in our physical world known to us as reality. I got my wish...I became pregnant!

As Buddha once said, "What we are today comes from our thoughts of yesterday, and our present thoughts build our life of tomorrow: Our life is the creation of our mind." So, now that you know the powerful Law of Manifestation, what will you begin to create from your wish list?

****

The second universal law I learned is the *Law of Attraction*. We've all heard the phrases, "You are what you think," or "Like attracts like." I've come to believe these phrases are literally true. For example, if you are thinking negatively about yourself, your experiences in the present will be ones of disappointment and frustration. This is because negativity attracts negativity. Remember, all thoughts are vibrational energy and are able to take form and shape. The more negative the energy, the slower the speed in which it vibrates. That is why negative entities can attach themselves quite easily to a person with negative thoughts; they are vibrating at a rate that is easy to penetrate or hop on. As we know, when we're depressed, nothing seems to go right. Salesmen know this all too well. Whey they are having an off day because no one is buying, their thoughts begin to sour. After a period of rejection, they might begin to question themselves, "Is it me?" If they do, and doubt starts to plague their minds, an attraction of negative encounters will start to surface. Downright rudeness or disrespect will slap the salesman in the face, rather than ordinary sales rejection. If the negative thoughts continue for an extended period of time, then undoubtedly, they will enter into the familiar salesmen's slump. Unfortunately, they can stay at the bottom until the attitudes or thoughts change in an upward direction. Remember, a negative encounter with another negative person will always occur because like attracts like. "Misery loves company" takes on new meaning, doesn't it?

On the plus side, the Law of Attraction also works positively wonderful in our favor. How many times have we said, "I was lucky." Luck has nothing to do with it. You were happy, you were confident and felt great that day. You were at the right place at the right time, because that is what you attracted to yourself. You were vibrating at a high, energetic speed, and attracted high level guides to assist you. Whether you choose lack from negativity or abundance from being positive... it's all up to you.

****

The *Law of Karma* is the third universal law I have learned. Some may think it's "an eye for an eye" or a punishment for a misdeed in a prior life. It is more about cause and effect. For every action, there is a reaction. As you know, what goes up must come down. The statement I prefer is, "What goes around comes around." In Bill's and Sarah's past lives, we witnessed a series of negative patterns that created negative karma. However, once the patterns were released and resolved, then positive karma took over. Now that they are aware of karma and how it is created, you can bet that they will choose to live out their present lives in a kind, respectful manner. They know that their present actions will create a very positive karma tomorrow and in future lives to come.

I have also learned that karmic relationships are established along our path towards enlightenment. That is why I've said, "Souls travel together time and time again." God gives us a million chances to get it right or enjoy each other's company. For example, when we meet someone for the first time and instantly have a bad, uneasy feeling about that person, chances are we've probably gotten burned by that person before in a previous life. The same holds true for instant chemistry. We can like a person enormously and feel we can offer trust. The familiar feeling is returned as if we've met before. We probably have, because chemistry, really, is just two old souls reuniting.

Throughout my research, past life relationships continue on in the present. That is why I firmly believe we pick our parents. Most of the time they have been with us before. If they haven't, they have agreed to help us with a particular karmic lesson. It was all agreed upon by all parties, including yourself, before you were born. It is part of your Divine Plan.

If we are awakened to these universal laws, then we are not victims of circumstance, for we can truly create our destiny. Our choice becomes whether to acknowledge our role and create it or ignore the laws and pretend they don't exist. Let's be honest: change is neither easy nor fun. It's much more comfortable to stay in an unawakened state of routine. But did you settle? Did your dream die along with your courage? If you had to do it all over again, what would you do differently?

****

I had this exact discussion with my friend. She was in transition because her employer was letting her go, due to downsizing. She's brilliant in her field and knew she could get a new position easily. But when I asked her, "What would you really like to do? What do you love? What is your dream?" she couldn't answer. We decided to consult her higher self for the answers. The vehicle of choice was hypnosis.

A few past lives were revealed to her. In one life she was a lost white child raised by native South Americans. In another, she taught math to groups of poor children, and in still another, she was a nurse who tended to wounded soldiers. When God, who resides within, was asked to help us understand the connection to her present life, the following meaning was given: The white child raised by the Indians taught her change can be good; the math teacher showed her she made a difference, while the nurse touched her inner desire to be of service and help people in need. This insight proved to be exceptionally valuable because it confirmed a hidden passion which lay dormant, and undisturbed, forgotten by her conscious mind but not her soul. "I love children, and I've always wanted to help them but didn't know how."

Could these past-life memories make a difference in her path? I think so. I'm sure that's why they came up. God was trying to tell her that change is not necessarily all that difficult. In fact, if she works with children, she'll be satisfying her need to serve and help them. In other words, she'll be following her Divine Plan. If she's open to the laws, then opportunity will manifest because her heart's desire will be nurtured by passionate feelings. She will attract people and experiences that will help her along the way because like attracts like. Karmic ties will be rejoined with people who have worked with her before, and positive karma will be ensured because she's following her Divine Plan.

****

Is it possible? You bet it is! God gave us the freedom to choose. Sure there's risk, maybe even sacrifice. But think of all the possible wonderful outcomes if you choose to climb up the spiritual ladder and take the voyage. Like Forest Gump's mama said, "Life's a box of chocolate...you never know what you're going to get." But you'll never know unless you try. Just imagine if you took a chance and ventured out to live your dream, to follow your Divine Plan...God only knows what lies ahead.

CHAPTER TWELVE

CONCLUSION PART I

*W*here do I go from here? If I believe my mind's eyes, then I have seen through the looking glass. In my meditations I have projected into the future. A whole new arena has opened up for me. Is it a coincidence that I have three teaching degrees but never taught in their respective disciplines? I don't think so. I believe my blueprint destined me to become a teacher – but a metaphysical one; to teach other people like me how to discover who they truly are. I am to help them by teaching them what to do; how to open and listen to their soul.

Almost thirty years ago, my mind's eye had shown me a repeated vision: I am standing at a lecture podium speaking to large groups of people on "Divine Plans." I see myself leaving the podium and stepping directly into the audience where pairs of individuals are practicing spiritual hypnosis and healing on each other. I walk among them, listening and guiding. I am at peace and profoundly humbled by the wisdom of the spiritual depth of the students. I am excited and grateful to learn from them as well.

Whether it was my destiny or subconscious wish manifesting, the long-ago imagery became real. In the beginning of this book I stated, "Be careful what you wish – for it might come true!" Well, it did for me. And you never know for you... I guess it depends on what seed you plant today.

We are body, mind and spirit. Most of us are preoccupied on keeping our body healthy and mind sharp but forget or neglect our spirit. Ask yourself if this is true for you. I know it was for me; until I awakened and realized that listening to my own higher self was crucial to my existence. I hope after reading this book, you will be a little more enlightened and eager to start opening up to your own wisdom within; your spirit that guides you forward on your divine plan.

PART II

JOURNEYS THROUGH RELATIONSHIPS,

CHAPTER THIRTEEN

RELATIONSHIPS: The Way We Evolve

*A*fter thirty-five years of witnessing clients' past lives and the processing of how they relate to their present lives, I can unequivocally state, "Relationships are the reason why we incarnate." Most of us have specific lessons we want to accomplish, for example, self-love, compassion, forgiveness, humbleness, etc. Relationships are the vehicles we use to drive us during our divine journey of understanding and learning. There are highly evolved spirits who have already learned their lessons but choose to reincarnate once again to help others evolve on their spiritual path. All our lives matter, and as Edgar Cayce once said, "The only way to heaven is on the arm of someone you have helped." I believe we don't go to heaven, but rather "grow" to heaven.

Think about the people you have met in your life where you felt instant chemistry. You immediately were comfortable and at ease, possibly laughed a lot, and something inside you said,

"Yes, I can trust this person. I like them immensely." This person likely became a very close relation to you, a best friend, lover, or spouse. This chemistry is your soul recognizing the relationship with the other soul; two old souls reuniting. Perhaps you were siblings, a parent to the other, married, or traveled seas together.

The same is true for people you instantly do not like. They make you feel anxious, and uneasy to be around them. You may question, "Why am I feeling this way? This person hasn't given me any reason to feel this discomfort?" The reason is a spiritual one. It is a different feeling coming from your vagal nerve signaling "danger or use caution". The spiritual feeling is more subtle and yet there is a definite knowing something about this person doesn't feel good. Again, two old souls reuniting.

You may be asking, "I felt instant chemistry with my husband, and after a few short years we ended with a bitter divorce. How could I have been so wrong in my choice of a spouse?" You may not want to hear this, but you were not wrong. There was "karma" carried over from a past or many past lives that needed to be worked out by both of you in order to grow and evolve spiritually. There were specific lessons that you both needed to learn, and being each other's teacher was agreed upon by both of you before you were born. Meeting and experiencing this relationship were part of both of your divine plans. How you chose to deal with this hard lesson is what matters. Love and understanding, or anger and revenge; there is always a choice. You heal the negative karma by learning the lesson and then letting it go with grace.

Karma is neither good nor bad. It is "cause and effect" by our thoughts and actions. Negative thinking about self or another is just as harmful as a physical action. Our thoughts are living things, and they can hurt or heal. This is why prayer is so effective. Positive karma attracts love and meaningful relationships and experience into our lives. However, if you are thinking or talking badly about a person, they will feel it. They may not know where this "psychic attack" is coming from, but they will feel inner disturbance. Can you see how your personal negative karma starts to pile up? Now imagine if you were obsessive with your thoughts. Adding more fuel to the fire may feel good in the moment, but it is very destructive to your spiritual goal of growth. Yes, it is hard. No one is asking you to be perfect, not even God. It is the recognition of negative thinking and feeling and then canceling those thoughts that help you move forward. Not easy, but as my son says, "I am a work in progress." After all, we are human with character flaws and faults. Love is the only way through the jungle of human experience. And yes, your karma whether positive or negative will likely attract the same souls into your next life to experience a relationship once again.

****

Case Study: Laura – An Awakening Story

A woman in her late seventies booked an appointment to discover why she was lonely. On the day of her session, she arrived on time with an abrupt abrasive attitude. I didn't take any mind to it because at this point in my career I was used to all kinds of people and personalities. I also did not want to jump to any conclusions or judgments because we all have a back story.

Laura had a fine chiseled face and reminded me of the British actress Judi Dench. However, her body sat rigid and protected with her arms folded across her chest. She had a hard time relaxing at first but soon realized that if she allowed herself to listen to the suggestions of relaxation, she would physically benefit from her muscles letting go of tension. Upon questioning, she delivered a story of her husband leaving her with four children to raise on her own. She worked hard and disciplined hard. I soon learned that all four of her now grown children had detached from her a long time ago. This woman had no relationships of any kind. No siblings, cousins, children, or friends. Her only conversations were with neighbors who occasionally said hello to her. She had a dog whom she said was enough.

When I told her "To go where you need to go" she regressed to her early childhood, which greatly disturbed her. Laura went into physical distress and wanted to leave this scene immediately. I took her to a place of her own choosing, a safe place, where she then described in detail a mother who horrifically emotionally and physically abused her on a regular basis. It was not necessary for her to relive those moments in time for it was clear they were very vivid in her mind. When I asked her why her higher mind took her back to her childhood, she said she didn't know how to love.

Laura told me she married to have a husband and children who would love her unconditionally but concluded she was unlovable for all abandoned her. The only company she did have was the elderly ill mother she had recently taken care of with resentment and hatred. When the mother died, Laura was relieved but felt even emptier.

She experienced a few more past lives and then travelled beyond the gate into the "life between lives" state. She was greeted by her soul family or collective with whom she had great affinity and love. A wonderful reunion occurred with energetic hugs and pure joy. There were five in her group, and she recognized all but wondered why the one she loved the most was wearing a mask. After much fun and communication, she asked her dearest to take off the mask. Slowly this particular spirit uncovered herself to reveal Laura's mother's face. Laura screamed and cried, "How can this be? Why? How can you be so cruel? No, no, no!"

It took some time for Laura to calm down and listen to what this spirit of love had to say. "Don't you remember? You were the playwright who wrote your script to learn specific lessons of self-love, compassion and forgiveness. All of us told you it was too challenging, but you insisted that you could handle it. Your desire for accelerated soul growth was admirable but we knew it was going to be a very difficult incarnation. None of us wanted to play the part of your mother. However, when you came once again to ask me to play this role in your life script, I had to say yes because I knew how much it meant to you. As you know, we have a great love, and it is because of this love that I volunteered to go on this journey with you."

To witness this awakening was mind bending to say the least. I knew that specific and familial souls travel with us lifetime after lifetime, but this scenario of pre-planning life scripts offered profound healing. I was humbled, and Laura left my office with a new and deeper understanding of her own role and how to move forward. She realized that she didn't learn her lessons well and needed to change the circumstances around her with the time she had left. She was determined to contact her children and beg them for forgiveness. Laura learned that the only thing that matters is Love, and how well you Loved in your lifetime.

****

Case Study: Louise – A Worthiness Story

Louise was a very attractive, vivacious and successful businesswoman. She was in her mid-thirties, married with one child. She was happy in her career, friendships and extended family but miserable with her husband. She kept the marriage going for the sake of her child but stated that she wore an emotional mask pretending to be happy on the outside but hiding deep sadness.

Louise initially tried to save her marriage by keeping her physical appearance alluring, cooking his favorite meals, and suggesting date nights. Nothing seemed to grab his attention. They were two roommates living under one roof. Even when she found out he was having a long-standing affair, Louise stood frozen in quicksand for years. She could not leave yet hated herself for staying. Louise came to see me in the hope that hypnosis would help her.

Her higher mind took her to three different paths letting her know that each was a definite probability if she chose that direction. The left path showed herself much older, bitter, and depressed. She was still in the marriage, but she was left alone a lot. Her husband came and went and showed no respect by dismissing her. When they did communicate the conversation quickly turned into escalated arguing. Their home was unkept, outdated and dark. A very depressing future indeed. She began to feel physically uncomfortable and could not wait to leave this path.

The center path presented a calmer picture. Louise was again older, still successful at work, but living alone. Her child was grown, and she was lonely. She chose a path of non-relationship with a significant other due to fear of repeating the same mistakes. A quieter, safer life, yes, but without love or intimacy. She felt happier than the left path, but it still lacked "life".

The right path showed her standing in a kitchen that was unfamiliar to her. It was designed in a style that was appealing and bright. She said it looked new. She was talking to a man but could not see his face or hear his voice. Louise began to smile as she animatedly began describing how she felt about him. She loved this man deeply, and knew he was her husband.

When I brought her back to the entrances of all three paths, I asked her which path she was being guided to take by her higher self. Louise was guided by her reaction to all the paths and knew, of course, the right path was literally the "right" path.

Change was frightening to her as it is to most of us. But Louise decided to change her life when she literally was shown other options of what could be if she took the risk to be happy. She realized she was worthy and deserved to have a reciprocated loving relationship.

Louise updated me to let me know that the divorce was not easy. She held her stance by focusing and keeping a strong intention on what she truly wanted. What delighted me most was when she called to tell me she was married to the most wonderful man, pregnant, and lived in a home with a beautifully designed kitchen that was bright like the vision she saw so many years earlier.

Louise realized that living in a loveless marriage taught her valuable lessons of self-love and self-respect. She also realized that her former husband was a valuable teacher for her spiritual growth. She was able to leave by believing "Goodbye, Good Luck, and Have a Good Life." When she decided to change and commit, it changed everything. Louise was finally able to let go and manifest a relationship that lightened her heart and spirit.

****

Case Study: Tiffany – A Hidden Vow Story

Tiffany walked into my office as the epitome of an ultra-feminine woman. She was comfortably dressed in a beautiful floral print, stylish shoes and exceptionally pretty. Her personality was soft and charming, and she spoke in the same manner. Her desire was to lose the excess weight she acquired while pregnant. Unfortunately, Tiffany continued to gain weight each year that passed until the point it looked like she was about to give birth once again. She expressed that she could not understand how this happened for she believed she did not eat so much or so badly.

While in hypnosis, I asked her higher mind to give her the answer to why she put on this amount of weight when consciously she desired to be slim like she was in her past. She experienced a few past lives that gave her insight. However, the true awakening came when she travelled back in time to her high school years in this life.

Tiffany was a competitive track runner. She practiced every day and was quite good. The only problem was she didn't like it. In fact, she hated it. Her father was the reason why she was doing this.

Tiffany began explaining that she was very thin growing up. So were all the females in the family. It was an unspoken rule that had to be followed to be a member of this family. Out of duty and love for her father, she obeyed.

While pregnant, Tiffany had emotional freedom to explore foods that were forbidden. Being married meant that she wasn't under the rule of her father anymore. This meant she was liberated to eat and, more importantly, be loved for who she was instead of how she looked.

When I asked her if she was ready to release weight once and for all, to my surprise she said, "No." Deep inside she still held resentment about her father and wasn't willing to let go of this emotion nor the weight until her father passed. She said that she was fine with this decision because it was her own way of standing up to her dad, communicating in a physical way rather than owning her voice and speaking her truth.

Decades passed, and when her father died, Tiffany lost all her excess weight and never put it back on. She was true to herself. Her higher mind showed her the reason for the weight gain, and it was the emotions of her relationship that overruled everything. She made a vow to herself and kept it.

It is important to understand Tiffany really did love her father deeply. She respected and honored him and understood his underlining need to surround himself with slim beautiful women in "his" family. Both had the same lessons to learn; self-love and acceptance, and their relationship provided the perfect way to do this. Tiffany just chose to learn in a different way. Like Frank Sinatra's song, "I did it MY WAY,"

****

Case Study: Carol – A Revolving Love Story

Carol was a middle age married woman with a spark of excitement and confusion in her eyes and speech. She felt conflicted because she felt devotion to her husband yet mesmerized by a man whom she recently met. She explained they both were waiting in an airport due to a delayed flight. When their eyes met, a strange feeling began to arise. Since they were sitting next to each other a conversation naturally arose. She felt tingles on her arms as he spoke. She tried to dismiss her initial uncomfortable feeling about this engagement because "after all, it's just a conversation." But something more was happening. She knew it, and he knew it. They learned a lot about each other and discovered they lived in the same city, with similar childhood backgrounds and interests. When it was time to board the plane, Carol felt disappointed to leave him, yet relieved.

While on the plane, Carol began thinking about how lucky she was to be married to her wonderful husband. Memories started to arise, and this calmed her. However, anxious feelings infiltrated her mind as well. She saw in her mind a vision of this man telling her how he wished he had someone who understood, respected and loved him deeply. Then she saw tears fall gently down his cheeks. She didn't dare turn around to look in the back where he was seated. Carol thought she was going crazy.

Weeks went by and all she could do was think of him. She wondered where he lived and what he was doing. Carol became anxious with each passing day. She felt terrible that she could have such infatuated feelings for a man other than her husband. This is the reason why she came to my office. She wanted to release this enticing man from her mind; she just didn't know how to do it.

In hypnosis she traveled to a past life where she was a rich little southern girl. She experienced herself running after the horse and buggy her father was riding in. She screamed out "Papa, Papa, wait, wait for me!" He stopped the buggy and jumped off to pick her up and give her a snuggle squeeze. He told her she was his little darling and that she could not go with him. As she watched him ride away, she cried. When I asked her if there was anything else, she jumped into another scene in history.

Different flashes of random movie stills flashed in front of her eyes: A young soldier embracing his mother as he leaves to go to war. In another flash an older couple embraced while the husband reluctantly had to go with the other neighborhood men waiting for him, again to fight in a war. A third scene showed a beautiful young woman in a ballgown waltzing in a ballroom with a handsome soldier wearing a red uniform. She told me they were deeply in love and betrothed. Instinctively Carol knew she would never see any of them again. A deep sadness appeared on her face as she started to cry.

A second session revealed a scene at a nunnery. She was one of two little school-age girls who were inseparable. She, the quiet and "good" girl, her friend, the mischievous, outspoken and brave girl. Carol described different visions of the girls' escapades as they grew up to be young women. She wasn't sure if it was out of duty or faith in God, but they both became Nuns due to their circumstance in life. All they had was each other.

Suddenly, Carol began shivering as she described being in a makeshift shelter in the woods. She was freezing and quite ill. She was lying on the ground with a blanket made of leaves, weeds and vines covering her body as best it could. Her beloved friend went hunting in search of food. Carol didn't know how she ended up there, only that there was a war on, and they had to flee the nunnery. They both assumed this was the safest place to hide from enemy soldiers. A few days passed and she never saw her friend again as she died a hungry freezing death.

Deep sorrow penetrated her heart as a pattern of loss and grief emerged. Carol wailed the pain from the past out of her until there were no more tears left to cry. Once she was calm again, I asked her if there was anything else, she said yes, but was not ready to explore it yet.

Carol's higher mind produced yet another scene in history on a vineyard in Chile. She was the grown daughter of the owner and was exceptionally comfortable with her lot in life. This daughter was in love with her father's right hand-man since childhood; and he with her. Eventually the father agreed to the marriage because she refused to marry a more desirable and advantageous suiter.

The couple produced two children, and they lived on the vineyard. She saw them having dinner with her parents and everyone was happy, including her father. Then she described her dancing with her husband on the veranda. She was very happy. She said this was a life filled with love, and it lasted a lifetime.

In between sessions, Carol would update me with her emotional progress. She stated she experienced synchronicities by bumping into him in random places; Once in the quiet of a beginning snowstorm, in a big box store, while taking a long walk with a friend, and almost hitting his unseen car while following a truck to make a left. When she saw the back of his car it stunned her because her birth year was on his license plate; and his on hers.

Each peculiar unplanned meeting aroused her feelings of desire and affection for this man. She also knew it was reciprocated. An unspoken knowing would travel between their telepathic eyes. It was becoming too intense. Carol would have vivid dreams every night about this lover, friend, spouse, parent, child, and colleague. The faces changed but she knew it was still them. It was affecting her relationship and her health. She confided to me she thought she was going crazy.

He began calling her to just talk. He told her she was able to see inside his soul and it frightened him and yet comforted him, knowing that someone understood him so deeply. They decided to be friends, but the idea of being "just friends" was too difficult for him. When they would meet, sometimes his behavior was strange; being dismissive or argumentative with her. However, he would apologize soon afterward for fear of losing his "friend". Carol called for another session to hopefully get answers.

The final past life opened with her seated at an elaborate vanity with a gilded mirror. She described the gown she was wearing, and the way she looked in the mirror; beautiful and heartbroken. Her much older husband came behind her to fasten a new jeweled necklace around her neck. This was a gift he was excited to give, but she could care less. She explained it was a loveless arranged marriage that was forced upon her. She loved the stable boy who she grew up with on a neighboring estate. It was devastating for both when this marriage took place.

The lovers would secretly meet until one day she didn't show up at the designated time. The beautiful woman became pregnant and decided it was better to protect her lover by separating from him. This pregnancy was frightening because her much older husband had trouble with erectile dysfunction. He was never able to consummate the marriage. How was she going to explain the pregnancy? This is why she knew she had to protect her lover. She knew her husband would find and kill her beloved.

Out of desperation and deep sorrow, she committed suicide. The husband found out about the lover from his domestic staff. With great anger and revenge in his heart, the husband tracked the lover while he was hunting and killed him in the forest. This lifetime affected Carol more than the others. She said it was so intense and real for she felt every emotion. After allowing Carol time to release her feelings, I directed her to the afterlife where she was able to receive understanding on a soul level.

Here she learned that indeed each scenario she witnessed in her past life journeys were true connections with this man she now knows in her present life. Many of the stories showed deep loss and yet deep love. They have a soul contract. They agreed to come back together repeatedly to help each other grow in spiritual development. They were each other's teachers. She taught him how to open his heart to love himself and another. To give his love and freely without worry or fear of the unknown. She taught him how to take emotional risks. She also cracked him wide open to spiritual ideals, and an invitation to bring joy into his life through relationship.

He taught her how to open her heart to receive love. Prior to meeting him, Carol felt unworthy and not good enough. She allowed the significant men in her life to make decisions and dismiss her intelligence. He came into her life once again to teach her self-love, and the importance of being true to self. To stand up for her beliefs and know that she mattered and made a difference.

She saw them both raise their hands to touch the other's hands in a prayer position. She immediately knew they were eternal Spirit Friends. The relationship changes in each lifetime, but they have an evolving loving karmic connection that serves the greater good for both.

Carol updated me to tell me that the intensity of emotions dwindled down, and eventually they both went their separate ways. Carol's relationship with her husband improved greatly; and he attracted a loving woman who adores and "gets" him.

When we take the time to honor our relationships by acknowledging feelings, dreams, and "coincidences", then we will grow in spiritual wisdom. We get signs all the time, we just need to become aware; see what we need to see and hear and acknowledge what we feel. It is in relationship with others that grants us the wonderful opportunity to advance in our development and frankly be happier while participating in this life's journey.

CHAPTER FOURTEEN

PAST LIFE ABILITIES - PRESENT DAY TALENTS

*T*hroughout the decades of being a spiritual hypnotist, past life regressions have shown clients the extraordinary gifts they once, or many times utilized to contribute to their community, country or even just to survive. These talents are remembered as second nature to the soul. Perhaps they are in our cells and referred to as cellular memory. Some clients didn't have to "remember" for they were born with the knowing, or the motivation to learn and experience this gift, and are still using these talents on a regular basis. Other clients' awareness of these talents were kept hidden until the time was ready for the memories and abilities to be called up for specific reasons. The following stories demonstrate this concept.

****

Case Study: Duke – a Life Purpose Story

A handsome male college student walked into my office

with confidence. He wanted to up his game in the sport he played. He heard that great athletes used hypnosis to become the best, and he wanted to be the best he could be. Duke easily went into hypnosis, but his higher mind sent him to a very different path, and one he was not expecting.

He found himself riding a horse somewhere in the Western part of the USA. He said he was wearing clothing from the old west, but he wasn't a cowboy. He wore a hat and carried a few guns, and a badge identifying him as a law man. Duke intuitively knew he was a bounty hunter. He began to tell me stories of how he would ride for days or even months to catch his man to bring him in for the reward. His strong will wouldn't allow him to give up. He confided how he loved the thrill of the chase.

While traveling in and out of towns he made more income as a gambler and entered sharp shooting bets. He was very good at both and enjoyed it immensely. However, at times he became lonely and wanted an emotional connection; someone to love and be loved back. Duke wished for the comfort of a wife and children. He did nothing about it and buried these thoughts in his subconscious. Making money and having fun was more important. When they did creep back into his consciousness, he justified his feelings by saying, "I'm gone from my home for many months at a time, it's not a life for a woman to wait for my return." As he progressed into the future of that life, he did see himself settled down with a wife and family. Duke said he felt good about it and wished he did it sooner.

After we processed this lifetime, Duke became even more perplexed. He wondered why he didn't see himself playing his sport. He was confused why his higher mind showed him this bizarre lifetime where he felt and saw every emotion detail. He said it was so real, and asked if this really could have been true? I told him I believe it is, and that his higher-self, his God-Source within, wanted him to have this experience for his highest good. His higher mind made the decision that this Bounty Hunter Life was more important than gaining more athletic ability.

Duke then confessed that he did not know what to declare for a major. His priority was to make money and lots of it. He stated, "I suppose I should major in Finance." I felt an intuitive reaction when he said that as a definite NO but kept my mouth shut. I suggested he take a career test to identify his innate talents, abilities, and personal interests. He agreed when I told him I would help him by administering this test. A week later we sat at my kitchen table for a few hours and were able to total up the scores to discover answers. He was shocked that Law Enforcement was the highest score, and Finance was one of the lowest. Duke dismissed this concrete evidence and decided to declare his major in Finance after all.

Upon graduation he received an internship with a finance company. After two months he quit because he was miserable. Soon another internship opportunity came up in a law enforcement department. It didn't matter that it was unpaid; he felt driven. Duke applied himself beyond expectation; arriving hours earlier and staying late. The top brass took notice and decided to advance his career. He was sent to an academy to train and when sharp shooting came up, Duke scored 99% hitting bullseyes over and over again. He and the training officers were amazed at his innate ability for Duke never shot a gun before. He smiled to himself for he remembered his life as a bounty hunter making extra money entering sharp shooting contests.

Duke stayed in law enforcement while getting promotions. Almost thirty years later, he remains in this career which he loves. And yes, he is happily married with children he adores. He learned "this lesson" by getting married in his 20s and not waiting till he retired like the bounty hunter's life. His family is his number one priority. For him, making money is important, but secondary. For a life without love, is not living.

****

Case Study: Maureen – An Independent Life Story

In walked a woman with a beautiful, serene face and body language that matched her quiet beauty. She was in her early fifties and was curious to experience a past life regression. She stated she didn't disbelieve but had doubts. She wanted to see if there was validity to reincarnation so decided to book a session with me. Maureen described herself as highly intelligent, a "left brain" engineer type person, reserved, and comfortable with her alone time. She liked her space to think. She said she had strong opinions and convictions but kept them to herself.

In hypnosis, Maureen saw herself as a young girl of two who could talk but had a hard time answering my questions. It was interesting to see Maureen take on the voice and mannerisms of this child. I progressed her to an age that was important for her to view and have a meaningful conversation with me. She saw herself at age 10 walking to school in the streets of Paterson, NJ with her best friend in the year 1907. When I asked why this was important, she stated her best friend is now her current best friend in Maureen's life. I smiled as I thought, "Once again, souls travel together through lifetimes because of love."

When I asked if there was anything else, Maureen moved into a scene in Japan during the 12th century. There was political unrest in the streets; killing and revolting against current policies. She stated she was a young man and took shelter in his art studio which he considered to be his sanctuary. It was in a secluded section outside the main village. Very few people were physically located near him. He had his privacy and the ability to produce great ceramic works of art.

He was commissioned to create art for prominent families

and political figures of the day, including paintings on scrolls. However, this artist was imprisoned and put to death for expressing anti-political views as symbolism within his art. He died swearing he would never speak out or release his deep convictions in any form, ever again.

When Maureen awakened from hypnosis tears ran down her cheeks. She explained she felt the pain and frustration from the artist, and confided she too sometimes felt triggered with fear when she would hear authorities discuss politics she didn't personally agree with. She began to look at the similarities of the male artist and her current life now. They had much in common besides personality. She had a very strong need to feel independent and free from judgement. Maureen had an immense need to feel personal freedom.

Another extraordinary connection was Maureen's artistic abilities. She was a gifted artist too who painted in a variety of mediums. She also experimented with jewelry making, and painting on fabric. She didn't know where these innate talents came from, all she did know was that she was in her joy while creating.

Maureen left my office with new clarity as to why she is the way she is and found great comfort knowing she is a woman of substance. She also gained an understanding of two personal truths: Love carries over from lifetime to lifetime, and so do our talents and gifts.

****

Case Study: Rosemary – A Desire to Be Famous Story

Rosemary was a world-renowned actress who was recognized by everyone on the planet. Stunning, beautiful and charming are words that accurately describe her. She had everything a woman could want except for the one thing she wanted most; a genuine reciprocated love.

She quickly entered hypnosis and described a scene in her childhood. She came from humble roots and felt secure. Early on when Rosemary longed to play and fantasize about another glamourous life, she would be told to stop daydreaming and get right back to homework or helping around the house. The dream of becoming famous never stopped. In high school she performed in many plays and continued through college. When I asked if there was anything else, she said, "They like how I look because I am pretty, but I am not sure if they love me for me." When I asked who, she said, "Everyone".

Rosemary then saw herself performing on stage. She was young and pretty, and part of the chorus; the group of players that sing and dance to enhance the plot. The show was presented in the early 1900s, decades before she was born. She loved the thrill of the audience and longed for recognition. Rosemary wanted to be a Star; but never became one. She continued to perform until she became pregnant unexpectantly and with great fear and dismay. Her ambition and career were ruined, but not her life. She knew most men were attracted to her so "getting" one to legitimize her was the easy part. Finding a man who she truly loved and knowing he felt the same was the hard part. Before the pregnancy was obvious Rosemary married a man she didn't love.

He took care of her because he was in love with her appearance and how he felt about himself with Rosemary on his arm. She was a trophy wife, and she accepted her position. Her dream of becoming a famous actress was extinguished.

When I asked if there was anything else, Rosemary jumped into a Southern Belle body like Scarlett Ohara, and in that timeframe. She had many suitors and appeared to be frivolous. She flirted and teased most of the men because it felt good. She knew she was somewhat attractive but not a beauty. Many suitors sought her father's fortune. Eventually her father chose the one she would marry. Rosemary lived the rest of her life in luxury but in a loveless marriage.

She then saw herself as a young maiden about to be married to a local farmer. She was very much in love and knew it was reciprocated. They lived quite happily for a few years until he had to leave; possibly a war or posse, she wasn't sure. She became very sad as she told me he never returned.

When we processed these lives, Rosemary realized there was a pattern regarding love, and a desire to be recognized for her talent. Her theatrical ambitions materialized in her current life, which gave her great joy. Every time she walked on a stage or television set, Rosemary became electrified as she electrified her audience. She knew she was greatly loved by her fans; and this helped to sustain her need for acceptance. However, her inward desire for genuine reciprocated love from a partner in life didn't materialize. Rosemary married five times trying to find the happiness she pined for. Again, the same pattern of men being attracted to her beauty, fame and money reappeared in her current life.

She reminded me of Marilyn Monroe. A great beloved beautiful actress who suffered the same fate. Rosemary, like Marilyn, needed to learn self-love and acceptance. Not depending on external factors or people to validate their self-worth. Ironically, the love from the audience gave them at least some comfort knowing they were truly loved; at least for their remarkable talent that began in other lifetimes.

****

Case Study: Three Little Boys – Future Life Stories

I was asked to babysit two little boys for a full day when my son was very young himself. Between the three of them I had my hands full. I could not do anything else but just be and be silly with them. After TV, coloring and games we all got tired.

I told them, "Let's close our eyes and pretend we are taking a nap." After the giggling stopped, I realized all the boys were in trance. I have always said, "Imagination is inspired information", and it was their wonderful imaginations that led to extraordinary discoveries.

I suggested they imagine who they were before they were the boys they know now. The stories they told one by one were interesting and sometimes funny. For they heard the other boys speak and then giggled; while remaining in a deep relaxed state of being. When I asked them to travel into the future of this current life, the boys became serious and matter of fact.

My son saw himself as a man with healing hands but used his voice and written word to heal others. He knew he was making a difference because people gathered to hear what he had to say. He didn't know how or what he was saying, but he felt it was important because it mattered.

Randy, the next eldest boy, saw himself as a teacher. He described that he loved what he did because it made him feel good about himself. He said he did not work in a classroom which confused him. However, he knew he was definitely teaching something, to whom he was not sure.

Dillon was the youngest; perhaps kindergarten age. He became very animated and yet adult-like when he described his future as an astronaut. He said his work was very important because he and his team were changing the weather. (This surprised me because this day with the boys happened in the 80s, and I knew of no such things.) The two other boys opened their eyes to look at each other and roared with laughter while Dillon ignored them and remained in hypnosis.

When I gave the instructions to open their eyes and feel good and terrific about themselves, they had lots of questions. They wanted to know if it was true. I told them they each have a higher mind connected straight to God within them, like a "Wisdom Wizard". Only this Wisdom Wizard knows the truth to everything, and all the answers they seek because the Wisdom Wizard and YOU are the same. And YOU deep inside, where the Wisdom Wizard resides, always know the truth. They nodded in agreement because they easily understood.

Fast forward decades later; all three men's visualized futures became manifested. My son has healing hands. He studied massage therapy and Reiki but decided to become an advocate for people with special needs. His public speaking and writing skills have produced quite an accomplishment for this underserved community. By being visible with his passion, he has made the invisible people become more visible too.

Randy is highly successful in business as a Corporate Regional Manager specializing in organizational behavior, development and training. Part of his daily duties include instructing employees how and what to do to improve productivity. He uses analytic, creative, problem-solving, and strong communication skills; just like a teacher.

Dillon is a high-ranking officer in the Air Force. He has moved up the ranks quickly due to his commitment, integrity, intelligence, and strong emotional quotient. Dillon is not an astronaut, but he was one of the first to be asked to join the Space Force Program. I have no idea what he does, but it will not surprise me if he has something to do with the weather.

All three men had a glimpse into a possible future when they were very young children. I believe our future is not set in stone for there are always detours we sometimes take from our divine plan. Of course, free will can change our minds and direction at any time as well. However, the three young boys' conscious minds chose to listen to their higher minds, to activate their divine plan, their blueprint for their current incarnations.

Their talents and natural gifts they were born with came from past or parallel lives, or possibly channeled from a higher being or collective to serve the greater good for all. This is true for all of us. Sometimes we just must believe in something beyond our physical body, and trust that inner voice inside to lead the way.

CHAPTER FIFTEEN

LIFE IN THE LIFE BETWEEN LIVES

I first met Dr. Michael Newton, author of "Journey of Souls" - his first book in a series to describe his fascinating research in the life between lives, at a book expo. My publisher introduced me to Michael when he stopped at our booth. I was excited to meet the man who explored through hypnotized patients what happens after we leave our bodies at death. Michael asked me to walk down the aisle with him to continue our discussion. I was glued to every word and then shocked when he told me he was about to retire. I pulled his arm and looked straight into his eyes when I said, "Michael, you can only retire when you have trained other hypnosis experts to do what you do. Your work is too valuable to get lost or forgotten with time. Teach a class and I will be the first one to sign up!" A year later, I was invited to join his first class in Virginia Beach.

I went with my good longtime friend, with the nickname "Frack". As Michael Newton lectured, we took frenetic notes and periodically would look at each other with eyes that said, "Really cool". One night our homework assignment was to hypnotize our study partner, follow the exact steps of his system, and record the experience in our notebook. I was hypnotized first, and my experience was wild. My memory of the event is minimum, but Frack took meticulous notes. She said I was introduced to my soul family, the Library of Records where I drew a specific emblem that appeared on the cover of my soul book. I just remember it had something with wings and fire on it. I then proceeded to tell her in a Spock-like voice and engineer character that my purpose in this dimension was to transmute negative energy to raise frequencies of specific incarnated people on Earth. I told her that while my incarnated body as Debra was sleeping, I would travel out of body to the person I was assigned to raise the vibration. I said I did this every night, for it was part of the divine plan. Frack said while I was speaking, I was very matter of fact and serious about my work. There were other like-minded souls who did the same work. We were a collective who were passionate about this project we agreed to be a part of. I said I had free will but there were higher level guides who were instructing us who to work on. Apparently when I left Debra's sleeping body, I somehow manipulated the astral fields of the sleeping people I travelled to; ridding them of disturbing elements that did not serve their highest good; and restoring balance before I left them.

Frack told me I was using scientific technical vocabulary describing what I was doing. It took everything out of her not to laugh because she knows how "right brain" I am and considers me an intuitive creative type with an odd sense of humor and tending towards being ditzy. What she was witnessing was the opposite of my personality. She said it amazed her. Upon reflection, it explained why I would wake up feeling exhausted. I guess I was literally slamming back into my body from my nighttime job.

What Frack and I learned in Michael's class, is that Life Between Lives is a real dimension for all who have incarnated and go there when we physically die. There are various levels within this dimension; "In My Father's house are many mansions." Projects we choose to work on to enhance spiritual development is just one of many activities or learnings. The ways to grow are endless.

CHAPTER SIXTEEN

DEPARTED LOVED ONES:
How They Visit

I have been fortunate to witness thousands of reunions over the past decades. Many occurred during hypnosis with clients, others were visited in dreams, given signs, or experienced actual physical visitations. There is no doubt in my mind that our loved ones continue existing.

Our loved ones have agendas like we do. It's all about spiritual growth through the purity of love. Hypnosis is a window of opportunity for a loved one to come into a client's mind to be able to say what they need to say. Most times the loved one's words are encouraging and loving, but sometimes the spirit is asking for forgiveness.

Most living people will feel their loved one's presence, or hear the voice, smell an aroma associated with them, or receive guidance telepathically. A beautiful healing usually occurs;

however, the clients always have free will which gives them the choice to accept or deny the message from a loved one.

Visitations, as I mentioned, come in many forms outside of hypnosis. Dreams are also an easy way to reconnect. As we sleep, our spirit body can leave our physical body at will to travel and go wherever we want. Clients have reported they experienced very realistic dreams of a loved one(s) where they were having a conversation while walking, sitting at the kitchen table, or just had ethereal eye contact that sent love back and forth. Very simple environments with extraordinary feelings of realistic connection; certain in the moment their loved one(s) were very much still with them. Upon awakening, they pined for the dream to continue for they knew it was something more than a memory; they were aware on a conscious level that their loved one came to visit them. Perhaps for comfort, advice, or assurance that they were still loved and "watched over" by them.

Signs are another way to let us know our loved ones are with us. The signs are many, ingenious and highly personal for us to recognize. Birds, butterflies and dragonflies are highly common; especially when they act unexpectantly by coming close and landing on our shoulder or finger or circling around us multiple times. My good friend, a widow, lets me know when her husband visits because he sends a specific summer bird during cold winter months to knock at her window when she is sitting by it. When my brothers and I performed a ritual for our mother's death, butterflies and dragonflies circled around us. Many people also associate cardinals with loved ones visiting them.

Some people find coins in unexplained places. After my father passed, my son kept finding pennies. Of course, I told him, "Pennies from heaven". On the day of my dad's memorial service, I watched my son squirm and make distorted faces as he walked down the stairs in his suit and dress shoes for the occasion. When he got to the bottom step, he flung off his shoe and there was a penny in it that caused the discomfort and recognition of my dad's great sense of humor and connection as loving Gramps.

Our loved ones want our attention any way they can get it, so it is important to be aware of what you were thinking because sometimes the sign has to do with our thoughts. I was driving home from a girls' getaway weekend on the Garden State Parkway. It is important to know that trucks are not allowed on this NJ highway. Because it was very early in the morning very few cars were on the road. I found myself thinking about my mother who had Alzheimer's but still recognized me. I knew she was rapidly declining, and I said to myself, "I do not know if I have the strength to go through another void." When I looked in my rear-view mirror, I saw a truck speeding up behind me. I thought, "Why is this truck on the parkway...he is not allowed on this road, and why is he driving so fast?" When the truck looked like it was going to kiss my bumper, it moved to the right lane. As it passed me, I thought I would naturally look at the driver, but I was distracted by what I saw on the side of the truck. In big bold letters the name ELLIOTT with a starburst above the last T was the "sign" on this truck. Elliott is my dad's name. As I drove in shock, I realized "Calling All Angels" was playing on the radio. I began sobbing. Then I heard my dad's voice say, "What void?" At this point I had to pull over to control my sobbing before I drove again. I was overwhelmed with all kinds of feelings, love, relief and pure joy. My dad's personality is bigger than life and very theatrical so it made sense he would "orchestrate" this very dynamic and physical sign. My mom, on the other hand, was the opposite in personality from my dad. She has come through with discreet subtle signs; hearing her voice and message in meditation, a feeling of her presence, or anything in nature because she loved the natural world.

Many people visit a medium to receive communication from a loved one. This can be very comforting and supports the living person's journey to carry on, knowing that their love is never separated; just different until they are all reunited in spirit once again.

CHAPTER SEVENTEEN

AKASHIC RECORDS: Checking In

*A*s I mentioned, I do not direct the hypnotized client where to go. I tell them, "Go where you need to go, and always for your highest good." Many times, after viewing or experiencing several past lives, clients find themselves at a gate with a gatekeeper. This is a doorway to the Life Between Lives. Usually, a guide or a loved one is there to greet them and then proceeds to direct them to the Akashic Records also known as the Hall of Records, or Library. This is a place where every soul's thought, actions, lifetimes - past, future and current have been recorded since the beginning of time, including all prebirth blueprints that each soul creates prior to incarnation. This blueprint or play is created by the soul, the playwright, to include all necessary themes, plots and main characters for the upcoming life. For each journey back to earth, a new blueprint will consist of lessons, missions, innate talents, and significant events to propel soul growth.

In the library, the hypnotized client can review their "book of records" and see how they are progressing. It is here where the client processes the specific past lives they just witnessed, by gaining clarity as to how those experiences connect to the present incarnation. Intense awareness of lessons and soul missions become keenly apparent. The soul of the client can measure how they are doing according to their blueprint, their divine plan they created.

Learning from the Akashic Records is an eye-opening experience, and sometimes a humbling one. We see everything, including the people we have hurt with our words and deeds. Some clients have felt the emotions of the other people as their own, and it becomes a valuable teachable moment. We can review the karma that we created, as well as the karma we have healed. Again, knowing that karma is cause and effect, the client can see their role in creating disturbance or halting their soul growth, as well as contributing love and healing for others they may have no awareness of.

It is important to remember our thoughts, actions and deeds are live and always being recorded. The only judgement comes from our own Soul. Learning lessons and choosing to correct mistakes helps the soul get back on track to complete the planned missions as well. Awareness of Self and motivation is the key to Soul Growth.

Imagine what our world would be like if every person on the planet knew and visited the Akashic Records and often checked in for personal review. Perhaps then we all could experience "heaven on earth."

CHAPTER EIGHTEEN

SOUL FAMILY and COLLECTIVES: Inclusive Belonging

*O*bserving the fascinating journeys of my clients, I can report we do indeed have a soul family besides our loved ones we knew on our earth walk. They are souls who are like us in development, interests, and soul rank. They are usually few, six to 12; and resonate with us completely. They all have different personalities but are attracted to the family for common goals and of course, love.

The family can choose to work on projects together or work individually. There is free choice always, and each soul chooses the direction it wants to take. The projects are as varied as they are here in the physical body. However, all projects have the same desired outcome; to help others grow in spiritual development with love as the guiding force. Clients have told me they work as healers to help the newly arrived souls recuperate from a challenging journey on earth. Other clients help prepare and teach new souls, while others have reported they help souls who are lost in the astral field and need to be guided back home to God. There are those who work with children, animals, and the plant kingdom. There are others who work on scientific or technical projects to advance the development of humankind, and still others who explore other planets and galaxies as emissaries. Some become teachers and guides when they attain more purity of spirit. There are even enlightened souls who assist the negative or dark souls see the light and learn from the past so they can move forward. The projects are endless and diverse; and always a soul choice once you have reached a certain level in your soul development.

A soul collective is a much larger group which can consist of thousands or more with similar vibration and focus of intention. Like a very large extended family, the collective is in place for collective learning, projects, and support of individual projects. The group is identified by the primary color; a frequency that each member in the collective resonates with. Usually, this color is in the soul body's auric field and can be telepathically seen by all. In essence, "like attracts like" is demonstrated by the collective.

CHAPTER NINETEEN

DIVINE PLANS:
Lessons and Missions

*C*lients report they look forward to meeting in the collective for they are reunited with friends. It is in this reunion, where sometimes decisions to travel together are made. Each incarnating soul can ask another soul from its collective or family to incarnate with them if it serves the highest good for all. Soul contracts are made and inserted in their Divine Plans for the upcoming incarnated lives.

Most incarnating souls have lessons, but not all. There are highly evolved souls that come back to help humanity rather than learn from having a human experience. However, most of us reincarnate to learn self-love, forgiveness, patience, and other traits that humble and help us grow. There is also karma that needs to be addressed and balanced as well. As mentioned earlier, karma is neither bad nor good but rather cause and effect.

Reincarnation gives us the opportunity to learn and correct our mistakes from previous lifetimes.

Clients discover their lessons in the life between lives state. Most report they become aware of their progress like seeing a barometer and hearing guidance. A big part of that lesson is to learn we are all connected, we are all one, and one with God. Invisible cords connect us all. This is why Edgar Cayce said, "The only way to heaven is on the arm of someone you helped." When you help another, you are helping yourself as well. I add, "You don't go to heaven, you GROW to heaven." The whole point of reincarnation is growing love; inside and out, and missions are the way we do it.

How thoughtful of God to give us the free will and creativity to also create meaningful purpose in our lives to feel joy while we do our earth walk. Any innate talent combined with a passion creates a mission. And they are as numerous and varied as our projects in the life between life states. Missions are a soul expression of who we are and what matters most to us. It doesn't matter if we create works of art, books, teaching, inventions, heal others, protect, serve, champion the underdog, rescue animals, volunteer, or have athletic finesse. What matters is how it affects others while we are sharing who we are. Some missions are huge and serve the world. Other missions are highly personal and serve our family as a beacon of love and light. Being an authentic role model that truly demonstrates love, kindness and respect for self and others is a great mission, simple yet powerful for its ripple effect. For many of us learn from examples.

Hypnosis is one way to discover your lessons and missions. Interpreting your astrological natal chart is another. When you write your divine plan in the life between lives state, a physical blueprint is also created in the stars. Planets represent core parts of the personality. Each planet has a positive and negative association with it. Think of colors. Red is physical energy or excitement. It also represents anger. Blue is calming and sad. Yellow is happy and fear. Traits of each planet are interpreted by the connections or aspects to other planets. It is these connections that can be positive or negative. Signs such as Leo, Aries, Scorpio, etc., are in specific planets at the time of birth. Signs also give the incarnating soul clues to talents and challenges. Planets and signs travel through twelve houses representing different facets in our lives: birth, marriage, career, family, higher learning, etc. A good astrologer will be able to interpret your natal chart to help you understand specific lessons (challenges), and innate talents (mission) and timing through transits.

If this sounds too difficult or overwhelming, there are terrific free natal chart sites online that will create your astrological natal chart and give you an interpretation. Not as thorough as a professional astrologer, but it's a great place to start. You will need to know your exact birth time and place of birth.

http://astro.cafeastrology.com

CHAPTER TWENTY

DIFFERENT LEVELS IN THE AFTER LIFE

*H*ypnotized clients have described many places they have witnessed or experienced that were disturbing, peaceful, adventurous, profoundly blissful and enlightening. They are as varied as the religious beliefs here on earth.

Buddhists believe there are six realms consisting of rebirth and an existence which could possibly be human or gods, animals, ghosts and various degrees of hells.   Hindus believe in "Moksha". This is an existence that is reached through spirituality and freedom from human desires. Muslims believe in "Barzakh". This is a place to wait until Judgment Day. In the Latter-Day Saint religion, all souls will be resurrected and will go to any of the three "Degrees of Glory". In early Judeo-Christian times, beliefs in different realms in heaven; places of pain and torment; resurrection and reincarnation were the norm, and an awareness of seven stages in the afterlife was a truism.

In today's advancement in communication via the internet, reports abound of different levels or dimensions in the afterlife. These learnings come from people all over the world and from all walks of life. Accounts from near-death experiences, people who have died and been revived, visitations from loved ones, channeled stories of after death, and of course, hypnotized clients have given us reason to believe there are many mansions in God's house.

The following is my own belief system formed by my clients' experiences:

Once we leave our physical body, most see a bright light or tunnel. We travel to a gateway where we are greeted by a loved one, guide or gatekeeper. We spend time in recovery in some type of healing environment where we are visited often by loved ones and guides. When we are sufficiently healed, we take time to reflect on the life we just lived. Usually there is a specific guide to help us with our learning. We are then encouraged by this guide to go and experience what we need at this stage of our development.

It is here where most souls enjoy the splendor of heaven they create in their minds. Some refer to it as Summerland. There is much joy and reunion with family and friends. We create whatever environment suits our needs; and we create it with just our thoughts. You have your former etheric body and can be any age that you choose. There is your favorite food if that is your choosing, and it is created by manna; but food is not necessary. Thoughts are communicated telepathically. Everything is transparent. Most importantly there are schools or temples for learning. When you are ready to advance to the next stage in your development, you will go to a higher level or sphere.

Edgar Cayce referred to this level as a waystation in the star system Arcturus. An interesting concept of multidimensional levels is his belief in planetary sojourns. He believed that learning on other planets; also called sojourns, takes place between earthly lives. The astrological natal chart reflects such experiences from the planetary sojourns for it strongly influences the current lifetime on earth. These sojourns can impact a natal chart physically, mentally, emotionally and spiritually but they are urges; not definite affects for a soul always has free will. If a particular planet is strongly placed in the birth chart, it is an indication of a most recent experience and learning from that particular planet.

Not all levels are pleasant and inviting. People who have lived their earthly life not respecting the value of life will find they are lost in darkness for a while until they discover a commonality with others who have committed crimes against humanity. There are many levels depending on how evil the acts or behavior and thoughts of the departed. Attitudes of greed, arrogance, bitterness, resentment, cruelty, superiority, etc. will have different levels and so will the deeds that accompanied those ego-oriented beliefs.

These levels have developed from thought forms of the souls that reside in them. Most are tormented and tortured by their own thoughts which create a definitive reality. All their senses are heightened to the awareness of all who they have hurt. If they inflicted pain, they in turn will feel and experience the same pain but over and over until they have learned to grow in awareness of love and God and begin to demonstrate it.

Not all these dark levels consist of incarnated souls. Thought forms are real and alive. When there is an abundance of dark thoughts percolating, an energy of negativity is created and becomes quite horrific. It can take the shape of anything to induce fear and control. People might consider dimensions like this hell, but I believe hell is an energy created from evil thought forms. The only way out is through introspection; and moving forward in loving thoughts of kindness or other positive attributes that are needed to be infiltrated into the heart and mind. These souls are rescued by souls who become guides to them; for they have been in these dark places themselves and have been rescued by other guides who have walked in their shoes. Again, "The only way to heaven is on the arm of someone you have helped... You Grow to Heaven."

God gave humans the gift of free will. It is up to every soul to choose what they will create with their thoughts and actions. Like a loving parent, God lets us learn from our mistakes. It is only then that we can continue our development and growth and become enlightened along the way.

CHAPTER TWENTY ONE

ENTITY ATTACHMENTS

I did not want to believe they were real, but over the years I changed my mind. I learned about departed souls attaching to people through experience. Early in my career as a spiritual hypnotherapist only a few clients presented them to me. During a session it would be clear that the person I was speaking to was an entity rather than the client. The higher mind of the client gave me permission to help the entity who was attached to them. For some clients, there were many attachments. Once the entity(s) are convinced it is in their best interest to leave and be guided to the afterlife, the client is relieved of their influence and disturbance. In my experience, most entity attachments are lost souls; unaware that they have passed on. The ones who are aware have chosen to stay attached because the loved one is tormented with grief. There are others who have unfinished business, and still others who enjoy causing havoc.

Entities attach themselves to people who have no idea they are carrying excess "baggage". In session I always ask, "Why did you attach yourself to this person?" and the following are common answers I receive:

The body had tears in the aura due to addiction

The body and mind were weak with negative thought forms about self and others

The body belonged to someone I love or hate

This is my body, not theirs

****

Case Study: Michele – An enlightenment

A woman in her forties booked an online appointment to discover why her marriage was failing, and how she could change the dynamics in the family with her nearly grown children. When we met on Zoom, I noticed how beautiful her face was. This was all I could see because she covered up her entire body up to her chin with a blanket. This was her comfort level, and I had to just go with it.

Soon Michele found herself floating in a colored light. She was aware of her deceased grandfather and could see him clearly. She asked why he came to visit, and his face changed into an unrecognizable face. She called it a Demon. Her higher mind called out to Archangel Michael, and he directed her what to do. Michele asked if there were loved ones who recognized this soul, and to come bring him back to God with them. She sensed another presence, while she saw the entity leave. When she asked me, "Why did my grandfather's face change?" Archangel Michael explained to her through telepathy the existence of entities. Her grandfather's face was used to get her attention. Apparently, it was just the beginning of an important discovery.

I followed with "Go where you need to go, and always for your highest good." Again, she saw another face, but this time a little girl. A dialogue began between the two. The little girl explained she was very ill but was unaware why she couldn't find her parents. She was hurt, sad, confused and lost. Archangel Michael encouraged Michele to do what she did with the demon face entity. This time she told the little girl to call out to any loved one who loves her dearly, and who she knew was with God. The little girl's grandmother appeared, as Michele watched the precious reunion. The two loving spirits were off into the light as quickly within seconds. Michele witnessed and heard everything in detail. She was amazed how clear and vivid everything was, including all the emotions.

Again, when I asked where she needed to go next, another lost spirit came into her presence. This was a man who had no idea he was dead. He was annoyed that my client was attached to him! He said there were others with him who felt the same. After much discussion of me trying to convince him of his true situation, a thought popped into my head. I said "Look at your hands, are these your hands?" He blundered out, "No. Whose hands are these? I don't understand what is happening." I finally had the opportunity to explain that indeed he was dead and had left his own physical body. The reason he believed he was alive is because his consciousness survived death. "We don't die, only the body does, the vehicle that housed our soul and spirit. Your soul continues to house your senses, desires and thoughts; the essence of who you are. Your spirit is what connects you to God." When I asked if he understood, the entity said, yes and was willing to go to the afterlife. I told him to take the others with him. Michele instructed them to call out to their loved ones, and they all appeared. Archangel Michael explained love never dies. Our loved ones in the afterlife watch over us. When we cry out to them, it is when they can hear and see us; they can find us and guide us "home". Michele watched as they all stepped into a light and left.

These experiences puzzled her. She wondered why she was seeing and talking with dead people. She was hoping to experience a past life or something else. Apparently, her higher self had other plans that were more important. Archangel Michael told Michele there is more learning ahead for her.

He showed her a panoramic view of her childhood and current situation with her spouse and family. She instantly understood there were entity attachments around her husband. He had a long-standing drinking problem that affected their marriage and his relationship with his children. He bullied, was dismissive, and had a tone of anger when he spoke. Michele loved him deeply despite his temper and behavior. She wanted him to change and be the man she married. However, she knew she could not change him but felt if she could remove the pestering annoying entities who thrived on her husband's addiction, then perhaps there was a chance for him to recover.

Michele was beginning to understand why she was presented with these entity experiences. She was told by others she was a healer, but did not want to embrace it. Her self-esteem was low due to the excess weight she packed on over the years. When she viewed the panoramic screen once again, Michele realized there were entities attached to her as well. She intuitively knew they became attached to her when she was a child experiencing fear and anguish due to abuse. As she grew, they grew. Michele said her inner thoughts of shame attracted them. Archangel Michael said, "You know what to do. You've done it before, and in other lifetimes. You are a healer. This is just one form of healing that comes quite naturally and easy for you. And you do it well because you utilize all your inner senses. These are gifts to help not only others, but yourself. Use them now." Michele did and when she was finished, she felt so free and "light". Archangel Michael reminded her that God gave us all free will, and the ability to truly be the Master of our own souls. With truth and firm conviction, Michele decided to step up to her true divine plan and love herself completely.

CHAPTER TWENTY TWO

ANGELS, GUIDES and TEACHERS

*T*here are hundreds of true encounters with these loving higher beings. They are present behind the scenes of our lives, cheerleading or supporting us every step of the way. The many types of ethereal helpers are vast and dependent upon what we need at any given moment in our life. Some of us are aware of our unseen helpers, but most are not.

Once when I was in a parking lot, standing in the back of my car with my trunk open, a woman driver backed out of her parking spot oblivious to me. Her car came literally inches from my body. The scene appeared in slow motion to me. Crazy as it seems I remained calm and unaffected by the near death. She, on the other hand, had a reaction of shock as she burst into tears. I found myself calming her down and left the parking lot only after I saw she was okay to drive again. As I drove away, I wondered how and why this event took place. As soon as I had that thought, a truck passed me with a painting of Archangel Michael with a sword. I didn't see the lettering, just the painting. I smiled at the recognition that I was saved by an Angel and began to offer prayers of gratitude.

In my practice I have heard or witnessed many angelic visitations. Some of my clients received grace, comfort or guidance. Others received protection the way I had. I now understand that Angels have never lived in a physical human body. Their purpose is truly to be a messenger from God. When we humbly pray, our prayers are heard, and a specific angel comes to aid. There are all kinds of angels, and a hierarchy exists in the angelic realm. These unseen helpers are miracles to us, and I believe we literally could not exist without them. I can only imagine how busy they are trying to balance our world right now. Thank God that they do.

****

Guides are vast and multiple too. They have lived as human beings and experienced the challenges and triumphs as we do. They walked in our shoes and know how to "guide" us in the right direction. There are business guides, creative guides, personal guides, etc. Each was assigned to us by their guides. By helping us, a spiritual relationship is formed. For as they guide us to evolve, we are helping them as well. We attract guides who align with us in development and interests. "Like attracts like." Some of our guides stay for a lifetime, while some are temporary connections. They assist us in any way that is for our highest good, and the highest good for all.

Clients receive the names of their guides and can describe what they look like. Their guides accompany them on their spiritual journey of self-discovery. Both client and guides are thrilled to make this "seen" connection. After the hypnosis session, the client can easily make contact when the need arises. The noticed bond develops, and life seems easier knowing we are not alone.

In 2016 I was inwardly pushed to paint deceased astonishing healers; Lew Smith, Ambrose and Olga Worrall, Bruno Gröning, and Edgar Cayce. As I painted their separate portraits, I could feel their presence. In self-hypnosis or meditation one of them would come for a visit to tell or show me something important.

Lew aka "Uncle Lewie" has shown me obvious physical signs which still awes me today. One day I asked him to meet my dad and my grandfather "Pa". The same afternoon while driving, a truck pulled up beside me on my left to wait at the same streetlight. I was shocked and thrilled to see "Elliott-Lewis" written on the side of the truck. Once again, Dad orchestrated a physical sign but showed me he met "Uncle Lewie". When Lew visits, I can feel him standing behind me with his hands placed on my shoulders. I will then hear his guidance clairaudiently, with my mind's ears. Lew Smith was a famous decorator in Miami during the day, and psychic/medium/healer by night. When his need to help thousands became too large, he left his decorating business and focused on his true calling day and night. People would knock on his door or call him all hours of the night. Lew had a great push to help as many people as he could, and his results were miraculous. He was able to physically hear and see all his guides at any given moment. He followed their instructions exactly and this is what produced the miracles. Lew's healing techniques were quite different than what we know today, for they were ahead of their time. He worked by changing the frequency of the disease or disturbance. We know this because Lew kept meticulous notes on every person he worked with, and every dialogue with guides and teachers which resulted in thousands of pages. I feel so honored to feel a personal connection with this extraordinary humble loving man.

The Worralls had incredible gifts of psychic mediumship

and spiritual healing ability. They offered their services to the congregation who visited the church, New Life Clinic in Baltimore, where Olga was the director. The couple worked together for decades as healers and founded the International Spiritual Frontiers Fellowship. Physicians sought Olga's aid both personally and professionally. She became a recognized national spiritual healer and there are books written about her and Ambrose.

Olga visits when I am troubled or worried emotionally. I hear her with a slight accent and a soothing voice. I feel warm healing hands placed on my heart which calms me enough to hear what I need to hear. I am greatly comforted by her presence.

Bruno Gröning is another interesting healer. In Germany after World War II, Bruno would stand amongst tens of thousands of people and send spiritual healing rays called "Heilstrom" to them. He said, "Trust and believe that Divine power helps and heals! God is our greatest physician. When I am no longer with you in person, everybody will experience help and healing from within. Everybody will be his own physician." He believed that if you asked God to send you the healing rays, he would send it. He instructed to never cross your legs or fold your arms while receiving the "Heilstrom" for it would short circuit the energy flow.

However, the mental attitude was much more important. Bruno stated, "Put what is evil (the illness) which has crept into your body behind you mentally and pay no more attention to it! Focus your entire attention on your healing! Now ask for the Heilstrom and concentrate on what you feel in your body! One person may feel warm, another, cold. The next person may feel a tingling in his hands and feet, or he may feel pain. This is Heilstrom and what you feel now has no longer anything to do with illness; now every sensation is a step towards your recovery. Your body is beginning to re-adjust itself."

Decades before I painted Bruno Gröning's portrait, my mother became painfully ill and needed surgery. The recovery process would even be more debilitating and painful than the surgery itself. Since my mom was a talented artist, I suggested that she paint his face with his expressive eyes "talking" to her. As she painted, mom said it calmed her fear while relaxing her body. She went into surgery knowing that all would be well. After the surgery mom experienced no pain. Her recovery was quick and comfortable. What was interesting was that mom knew nothing about Bruno. She kept his portrait on her dresser facing her bed. It was her faith and the power of the suggestive words from Bruno that gave her what she considered a miracle healing.

Edgar Cayce is probably the most recognized of the healers I painted. He had the uncanny ability to enter a somnambulistic trance quite easily and then access his higher self to assess an ill person's condition and provide not only a diagnosis but exact method for healing. Edgar stated that he was unaware of the teaching or diagnosis that came from him while in this "sleeping state". Physicians and people from all walks of life requested a reading from him for decades.

While in trance, Edgar would speak on a variety of topics; reincarnation, the afterlife, nutrition, astrology, past lives, healing, dreams, the future, etc. Whatever was asked of him, he was able to supply an answer. He believed these answers came from his subconscious mind which was connected to all minds while in trance; tapping into a collective consciousness.

When I choose to enter self-hypnosis for answers to questions, I have about self or clients, I have found Edgar Cayce to be a reliable great source. I telepathically receive the answers. I feel he is a healing guide that helps me when I am helping others.

****

Loved ones who have crossed over may choose to be

personal guides to us. They can easily hear us talk to them, and as I mentioned they show signs to let us know they are near. Having a conversation with them is easy. When you are quiet and in a place where you are undisturbed, center yourself with a few deep breaths. Say a prayer and ask for the loved one you would like to talk to. Start a dialogue with a question. Listen to the response. Listening can come with hearing their voice in your mind's ears, or from thoughts you receive through your own reading voice. Perhaps you will see images or symbols in your mind's eye with a "knowing" of the correct interpretation. You might have a strong feeling or hunch. Our loved ones have peripheral vision. They can see what we cannot. They are not all-knowing advanced higher beings, but they perhaps know more than we do about a particular circumstance. It is their love for us that motivates them to continue the relationship. If they can help, they will, but only for the highest good for all. They will not interfere with your free will or karmic path. However, they will support, encourage, and provide guidance if they can. You will know your loved one is present by how you feel. Believe they are only a thought away, because they are.

****

Teachers and Master Teachers: Just as guides come in during various transitions in our lives, so do Teachers. They are higher level beings concerned with our spiritual development and help us in learning from our negative karmic lessons we wrote in our life script for the present incarnation. Like academic teachers, they understand our conflicts and challenges. They encourage us to learn from our mistakes and then do the right thing whatever it is to "balance" the scales. Teachers celebrate with us when we learn and move forward.

My son, Nick, had a spirit teacher for many years while attending elementary school. She told him her name was Barbara and she was there to help him pay attention. Every time his mind would wander with something that distracted him, Barbara would tap him on the shoulder and say, "Pay attention please." For many years he would insist that she was real, and I believed him. She continued to accompany him during those challenging years of bullying and isolation from his peers. I know she helped him with self-worth and the ability to enjoy the company of his own pleasure; lessons he needed to learn.

****

Master Teachers provide support with our spiritual development but on a grander less personal scale. I imagine a Master Teacher to be like a respected college professor, and the teachers, their graduate assistants. They urge us to change our attitude or thinking by awakening to more uplifting and loving ideals. They teach spiritual principles for growth and understanding of God. They influence us to see and feel clarity of love, acceptance and forgiveness for self and others. A Master Teacher is attracted to the energy and character of our spirit, and I believe we are all assigned to one prior to birth.

One day when my son was just an infant, I obtained a sitting with a prominent spiritualist medium in Bluebell, PA. Joan was extraordinary in her skills. She brought in very specific details about my grandparents, and other family members who had passed. She spoke of life events in my childhood that brought instant clarity and healing for me. I watched her speak to them as she communicated the messages. Joan was then instructed by my Master Teacher, Master Abraham, to allow him to speak directly to me. He had much to say about spiritual matters and how I was doing in that department. He offered suggestions that would help my spiritual understanding grow. He also told me that Master Samuel was my son's Master Teacher. I was indeed humbled that day.

If you want to know who your Master Teacher and teachers

are, meditate. Sitting in quiet, in time, quiets your thoughts to hear them. Set your intention, say a prayer and ask for them to come. Start by asking a question and then dialogue. It will feel like your imagination, but remember, imagination is "inspired information." Trust in what you receive. Thank them for coming, and finish by journaling if you choose to do so.

Know that you can do this with your guides, loved ones, and higher mind too. It's just one way to get in touch with your own spirit and the spirits of others who love you. Just remember to ask for protection and loving guidance before you begin. Higher beings will always give you encouragement and loving support. They will never tell you "You MUST do this and that..." for they will not interfere with your free will. If you hear directives or any negative thoughts, know this is not a communication from spiritual higher beings. Recognize how you are feeling and know what you know.

When you think of loving thoughts, you feel good. You know this. The thoughts generate love throughout your multi-level bodies; physical, etheric, mental, astral or emotional, and celestial. As your frequency increases, so does everyone you encounter. It's a domino effect. We are all connected, for we are all One. This includes the spirits in the afterlife. Love; radiant love, is the only way.

PART III

EXPERIENTIAL EXERCISES

CHAPTER TWENTY FOUR

AURAS

I first began seeing auras while attending a business lecture during my early days of awakening to metaphysics. I don't know if I was tired or bored with the program, but I soon found myself politely watching the speaker while my mind wandered elsewhere. Twenty minutes or so had passed when a bright green impression surrounding the speaker got my attention. It surrounded his whole body and seemed to have a life all its own for it would fade, disappear, then illuminate once again. Like a dance, it moved with every step. I delightfully watched the progression of the green grow from small to large, then disappear. This light show was better than anything I had ever seen before. I was in total awe of what my eyes were seeing. I nudged my friend sitting next to me and wrote down that I could see the green around the speaker's body and asked her if she could see it too. She looked at me kind of strange and shook her head. I was disappointed that I couldn't share my new visions with her, but I was still thoroughly entranced with the remainder of the evening. I had no idea what the lecture was about, but that night I learned more with my eyes than I had with my ears.

The colors in an aura appear to be vibrations of matter that form a pattern. This pattern or blueprint is a three-dimensional picture of what our soul is experiencing in the moment, for it paints an accurate portrait of our physical, emotional, mental and spiritual states. It is a field of energy that resonates all of our thoughts, feelings, and actions, and shifts or changes as quickly as we do.

During the massage days, feeling the aura was quite easy. Sometimes I would see things, but since I was in a trance most of the time, I just decided it was part of my imagination. It wasn't until years later that I learned that what I was seeing was indeed the client's aura. As soon as I had accepted the fact that it was real, the colors were flying into my field of vision without any warning. This became really disturbing. At first, I was thrilled, and then later annoyed at my lack of control. I couldn't turn it on or off. Sometimes I would be watching Nick climb a tree and see him surrounded in the most gorgeous ruby red. It was so vibrant and alive. He really did look like a gem. Unfortunately, at other times, the light show was not so appreciated. I remember conducting a business meeting when suddenly green and blue started intertwining around an executive's head. It took every bit of concentration to ignore the dance of light and pay attention. I decided I had to take control over this new skill immediately. I had to learn how to bring it on at will. Since our bathroom had a full-length mirror with assured privacy, I would sit in there for long periods of time staring just slightly above my head. I found that not really "looking" but rather gazing out of focus brought me aura vision. As soon as I would see a color, it would vanish in an instant. The more I tried to focus and hold on to it, the harder it got. It's almost as if you have to not try in order to see it. It reminds me of trying to see those three-dimensional pictures that pop out at you, after softly gazing at a multi-dotted, non-descript picture. After a number of weeks of nightly trials, my aura vision finally was able to be somewhat controlled at will.

However, just being able to see the aura wasn't good enough. While working with clients I discovered that the colors would always appear in and/or around their bodies. I wanted so badly to be able to understand what the colors meant, but unfortunately, I couldn't interpret what I saw. So, I went back to reading as much about aura interpretations as I could. There are many experts on this subject, but the one I found to be most beneficial, because of his simplicity, was Edgar Cayce, the great medicinal diagnostic psychic of the past century. As a young child, Cayce saw different colors around different people. He assumed everyone saw them too. In time he realized that his ability was an extraordinary psychic gift that enabled him to interpret a person's true nature and condition of the physical, mental and emotional body. Connecting an aura and personality was a natural for Cayce as making an association between an ethnic name and nationality for us. He would watch the colors change as one's moods and health changed. Like the weather, Edgar Cayce was able to see and predict changes depending upon the color and shade that he saw.

He was determined to find out if his interpretation of the colors were correct. After consulting with other psychics and people who had experienced seeing it, he concluded that his own intuitive impression regarding each individual color was accurate.

For example, red in general would indicate that the individual has a lot of energy and vitality. However, depending upon the shade of red, it could mean something entirely different. Light red would mean that the person is nervous and impulsive, whereas dark red would indicate that the person has trouble controlling his aggression. "He saw red" tells us about the anger which an individual would be feeling. Scarlet, on the other hand, says "full of himself." Pink indicates innocence and adolescence as well as love and compassion.

Orange is the color of creativity, socialness, and courage. It could also mean laziness and apathy towards others.

Yellow is the color of mental activity and joy. Depending on the shade and mix, it could also indicate a frightened or indecisive mind. "Yellow belly" clues us to its negative side.

Green is the color of healing. Many doctors, nurses, and healers have this color in their aura. When this color is mixed with others, the meaning changes drastically. When blue is combined with green, it indicates that the person is helpful and can be trusted, whereas when it is mixed with yellow, the person is dishonest. "Green with Envy" is true when this color is cloudy.

Blue is the color of goodness. A dark blue signifies a spiritual, unselfish quality: people who are highly dedicated and devoted to their work. A medium blue shows a hard, loyal worker, while a light blue means the person is struggling towards maturing in a spiritual sense. When blue is muddy, it may mean the person is worried or feeling melancholy.

Purple or Indigo is the color of psychic energy. A person with this color in her aura would indicate that she is developing her psychic abilities or is a natural-born psychic.

Violet is the sign of a spiritual seeker. This soul is longing to connect profoundly to her purpose and God.

White is the color of perfection, something we all strive to achieve, for it is complete harmony and balance. It is the blending of all colors which produces a pure white aura. Many people who begin to see auras see white around the head. This is a preliminary stage to seeing colors and should not be mistaken as the perfect pure white aura.

Black is the color of protection or an indicator of an imbalance in the body. It is not a negative color but rather one that gives us clues to a disturbance in the physical body. It can indicate a problem in the early stages even before it has actually manifested in the physical body.

Again, it is important to remember that reading an aura is much more involved than just knowing what a particular color means. The depth, intensity, quality, location, how it intermingles with other colors, and its relationship to the other colors all need to be considered. Even the shape can tell a lot about the condition of a person. We are all constantly changing either progressing or retarding. Our aura will reflect the state which we are presently in and where we're headed. All these characteristics need to be interpreted accurately in order to fully understand and help the individual.

This aura diagnosis was quite fascinating but scary at the same time. Who was I to think that I could accurately diagnose what I saw, nevertheless pretend that I was an expert? So, I did what I always believed to be true and wise...asked the "psychic within" each client to interpret the colors that I saw in and around them. For they are the expert on themselves and know truly the answers that we seek.

During a session with a client, I will usually see a predominant color around his or her head and shoulders. Sometimes I will see it on the throat, eyes, stomach, or other parts of the body. After I describe what I see, the client will tell me exactly what it means. The responses are as varied as the clients. Sometimes it will be a desire, a warning, an idea...but always exactly what the person needs to know. It's like a light bulb that clicks in one's head, and he or she realizes, "So that's it!"

Sometimes color isn't part of the aura at all but the presence of a guide, teacher or loved one. The clarity and intensity of the color seen is always clear and bright, very beautiful to look at. Sometimes, however, the color is dark, drawn, and muddy, and I can usually feel it's heaviness in my left arm. Nine out of ten times, the client will report that the muddy color is an entity that has attached to their aura, and that this color is definitely not a part of them. In some instances, the client will state that the color is a thought form of his or her own making, or a thought that belongs to someone else. In this case, he or she is able to decipher the meaning quite easily.

It is obvious why I ask clients to interpret their own auras. They are always accurate and benefit greatly with their own understanding. However, it is much more difficult to interpret one's own aura. The best way, I have learned, is to trust in the response I receive in meditation. Sometimes I don't want to see or believe what I am picking up, but when I ask for guidance, I always receive. It doesn't matter if I don't like it; what matters is that it just exists. It is reporting to me the condition of my mind, body and spirit at the present moment, and in what direction I am moving. It's not the cause of who I am, but rather the effect of what I produce. How lucky we are that God gave us such a tool to use for our health, wellbeing, and development. We all have the ability to see and read our own auras, if only we use this gift. Like anything else, practice makes perfect. Just imagine thought, if we were all able to read ourselves and each other...where every thought and attitude were as clear as day. You couldn't possibly lie to yourself or others, for your truths and beliefs would be exposed. This clarity would force us to look at our world and our personal self with honest integrity. For the truth it delivers would wake us up to the real state we're in and where we need to focus and put our collective energy towards building a real brotherhood of mankind. Just imagine if our future was void of deception and disharmony.

I wonder if John Lennon saw auras or contemplated this thought when he wrote "Imagine." It's an interesting thought, isn't it?

CHAPTER TWENTY FIVE

FINDING YOUR OWN DIVINE PLAN

*I*f you find yourself restless, bored, or dissatisfied, maybe it's time to take a closer look at what you really want. Maybe it's your soul's way of telling you to wake up and take action. Sometimes we may be experiencing this uncomfortable gnawing feeling because it's the only way we'll listen to our inner voice. How many of us work in a job that pays the bills, rather than one where we feel passion? How many of us stay in destructive relationships because familiarity is more comfortable than taking risks? How many of us ignore that inner voice that wants to guide us to our true purpose and vocation because our belief system says it's impossible or we're just not good enough?

I too played the unawakened victim of our society until my wonderful clients and personal experiences taught me that there is so much more to our physical existence. I know now that there is truly a very specific reason why we're here and that each one of us has our own divine plan.

One way to access your own divine plan is by seeking advice outside yourself. This is how most of us begin to question our existence. Psychics and astrologers have been around since the beginning of time, but it wasn't until recently that the masses have been flocking to them. Is it a coincidence that psychic networks have popped up on TV and are making a fortune in the process? The demand for answers is upon us. People all over the world are getting fed up with the cold, materialistic side of modern-day life. A cry for spirituality and a new age of thinking is manifesting with rapid speed. It's a great time to be open to metaphysics and search for your purpose, for there are many external sources to help you. Psychics, numerologists, and astrologers are one way. Hypnotherapists, progressive psychotherapists, art, drama, and music therapists are another. Holistic centers offering workshops and lectures are other avenues. There are so many choices to initially spark you into examining your heart's desire.

In the beginning of your search, you may feel more comfortable joining a like-minded group or participating in a series of workshops. This is why initially it is wise to start externally – outside yourself. Once you've whetted your appetite...read, read, and keep on reading! The Internet may be helpful too. The key is to acknowledge that "questioning feeling" and begin your search.

When you have become comfortable with all of the information you've gathered, and feel you are truly ready to start exploring your inner world, there are a number of ways to access your higher self. I personally have been drawn to meditation, self-hypnosis, dreams, I-Ching, and the pendulum. Friends of mine swear by the tarot cards and runes. The instrument of choice is not what matters but rather the guidance you receive from within.

****

We all know what meditation is, but for the longest time I didn't think I was doing it right. It was so hard to stop the chatter inside my head; so many images would appear without rhyme or reason. I felt like a fool and questioned my ability. However, the feeling I would get from a meditative session would offer more clues than the actual experience. Once I decided to stop trying so hard for the answer, I just told myself to relax, and trust that guidance would come. Sometimes it did, and sometimes it didn't. I always felt peaceful and a sense that it's okay; that somehow, I wasn't ready to receive the message. Maybe my higher self knew that I would reject it if I consciously knew the truth. Maybe my body needed to unwind and balance on an inner level. I've learned to trust and let God, and his helpers help me. For my faith comforts me and allows me to believe that not only will I be given the correct answer, but I will receive it in the correct time, as well.

There's no effort anymore to meditating. It's a haven from hectic everyday life. All I do is put a peaceful piece of music on, sit in my recliner with a crystal, and ask God to relax me to where I need to be. That's it. I either go off on a mind journey anywhere between ten minutes to an hour or just drift off into a deep relaxation. Whatever happens, I know at that moment it is for my highest good.

****

Self-hypnosis is like meditation; they both bring you into a trance state. However, self-hypnosis is more guided rather than free flowing.

CHAPTER TWENTY SIX

EXPERIENTIAL EXERCISES

*C*linical Hypnosis Scripts are a general way for you to experience for yourself what it feels like to be self-hypnotized. All you need to do is read the script out loud while you record it onto your phone. Read with your most relaxing voice, slow and soothing. If you want to emphasize a point, please do so. You can read the script as is, or you can change it to first person using "I" instead of "You". This is your recording, and you know what you like and what is best for you.

HYPNOSIS INDUCTION

"Find yourself in a comfortable relaxed position and in a place where you will not be disturbed. Take a moment to really feel comfortable in your recliner, chair, sofa or bed. Take three deep breaths. Do this now. Inhale to the 4-count of 1,2,3,4 hold 1,2,3,4 and release slowly 1,2,3,4. Do a second 4-count slowing it down even more while pushing your belly out while you deeply inhale. And now the third breath....

I'm going to count down from ten down to one. With each descending number you become more and more relaxed. Without any effort on your part, it just happens because the breath takes you into a deep relaxed state of being. As you mentally count very, very slowly, you realize that you are starting to enter the deep relaxed state you desire.

TEN, deep, deep relaxation. The deeper you go the better you feel, the better you feel the deeper you go. NINE, more and more relaxed. Without any effort on your part, you easily drift off into a deep, deep relaxation. EIGHT, you may find yourself feeling as if you are melting down, down, down into the chair or wherever you are in this moment. It's a peaceful feeling so enjoy it. SEVEN, the deeper you go, the better you feel, and the better you feel, the deeper you go. SIX, down, down down. See or imagine yourself riding down, down, down an escalator. FIVE, more and more relaxed. Feeling good, feeling safe, feeling relaxed. FOUR, (pause and remain quiet for 10 seconds) relaxing even more than you were a moment ago. THREE, take another deep breath and let out a big loud sigh. Do this now. The breath sends you deeper and deeper into profound relaxation. TWO, so wonderfully relaxed, you can even go deeper. ONE, down, down, down into deep hypnotic relaxation.

If you would like to go even deeper, nod your head. Choose a finger on your dominant hand that indicates "YES" and raise it. Do this now. Each and every time you choose to go into deep hypnosis quickly, you will listen to this script until you memorize it. Once you raise your "YES" finger you will move even further into a blissful relaxed hypnotic state. Raise your "YES" finger again to confirm if this is what you want. Good.

Imagine you are walking in a field of beautiful wildflowers. Perhaps you can see the colors as you approach a collection of a particular variety that attracts your eye. Do you hear the sounds in this field? Buzzing bees, birds chirping or water bubbling? Can you feel the sun on your face or back, or perhaps a gentle breeze? Imagine you are walking barefoot. Can you feel the soft grass beneath your feet? Can you feel the petals of the flower? How about the aroma from the flowers? Can you smell the sweetness in the air as breeze blows?

Now you are ready to make positive suggestions for your subconscious mind to receive and implement. YOU are the master of your ship, and YOU are the only one who knows what is best for your highest good. Only positive and loving suggestions are admitted into your glorious, wonderful mind.

****

FOR UPLIFTMENT

Find yourself sitting with a special friend. Not just an acquaintance, but a friend who really loves you. This person "gets" you and understands your motivations. Cheers you on and cheers you up. You trust this friend completely, as they trust you. There is genuine reciprocity and caring. You are accepted and loved just for who you are.

Invite this friend to sit down next to you. Begin indulging in enjoyable memories of past events you shared together. Notice your friend's smile. Notice yours. A particular very funny story pops into your mind. It makes you laugh out loud just at the thought of it. Share this story now with your friend. Take a few moments to experience the memory. Do this now...... take all the time you need to really feel it. Notice how you are feeling after the memory was relived.

You feel good. You feel happy. You feel loved.

Now imagine another memory when you were being acknowledged for something you did. An accomplishment? Perhaps being recognized at work, or for a creative project, or deed you volunteered to do? Notice how you feel about yourself. Go back to this time and experience it further. Listen to the compliments. What are they saying? Does anyone shake your hand, pat you on the back or hug you? Connect with the positive emotions emanating from the experience of this memory. Do this now.

You feel good. You feel happy. You feel loved. I feel LOVE.

A third memory comes to mind. It's a time when you helped another person, and the outcome was joyous. It doesn't matter if they asked for your help and you willingly agreed to help them, or a random act of kindness. It is the helping of another that matters most. Let the memory emerge quite vividly now. Imagine you are telling your friend this story until you become the participant once again, vividly seeing it in your mind's eye. Hear the dialogue between you, or the sounds in your environment. Feel the emotions of you and the other person. Have the perception that you are there, right now, experiencing it once again as if it was happening in the present moment. Do this now. Take all the time you need.

Notice how good you feel. Notice how good you feel about yourself. Repeat and say out loud:

I feel good. I feel happy. I feel loved. I feel LOVE. I AM LOVE.

Say it again, out loud and with meaning.

I feel good. I feel happy. I feel loved. I feel LOVE. I AM LOVE, and I MATTER.

Yes, you definitely are love and definitely matter for you are here for a reason. Sometimes life gets messy, and we are faced with problems that upset us. These challenges are lessons that your soul chose to learn and demonstrate resilience and self-love. Know that at any moment you can choose your perception on how to deal with a circumstance. You are choosing now to feel good and happy, and acknowledge you are loved and loving, and indeed are LOVE.

Raise your right finger now and say out loud, "YES, YES,

YES. I AM LOVE." Yes, you are love. And that is why you uplifted your frequency today. Each and every time you repeat this uplifting session; you build yourself up. It's that simple, and that easy.

Now on the count from 1 to 3, you will make another decision. You can either remain with your eyes closed and drift off to sleep if you are prepared to go to bed for a blissful sleep for the night, or open your eyes and become wide awake, mentally alert, physically refreshed, and emotionally feeling so uplifted and ready for a terrific, wonderful day. 1...2...and 3. Your choice, blissful sleep or blissful day. Know you are uplifted and have raised your vibration in every way. God Bless You.

****

OPTIMUM HEALTH

You know we are more than just our physical body. In fact, we have many other bodies that are just unseen to the physical eye. However, they are just as important as our physical dense body. We will explore each body to see if any adjustments need to be made, for we desire and deserve optimum health.

Scan your Physical Body now. Allow your higher mind to shine a light on anything that needs your attention. Perhaps it will be a color or spotlight that illuminates an area in your body. Do this now. Perhaps you hear your higher mind tell you. Pay attention. Maybe you feel a pain or disturbance. Pay attention. Begin to dialogue with the body part or organ. Ask as many questions as you need to. Listen without judgment. Do this now. Ask your higher mind, "How do I bring back balance to heal?" Your higher mind is all knowing because it is a direct link to God. It is your wisdom within. Listen to the wisdom. (Pause) When you feel you have received clarity and confidence with your answers, say the following suggestions out loud: "My physical body is vibrant and healthy." "All my organs and systems are working in perfect harmony." "My mind and body connect lovingly and easily and in perfect sync." "Each and every day I get better and better." "I trust in the process of healing." "In each and every way I am well, safe, and grateful."

Take a moment and see how these spoken words resonate within you. If you need to repeat it, do this now. (Pause)

Your Etheric Body lies closest to the physical. It is an exact replica of your physical body but in a subtle vibration. If there is any imbalance it will show up here first, before it appears in the physical if not corrected. Scan your Etheric Body now. Again, let your higher mind direct you by showing, telling or a feeling. If you sense "clearness", this is wonderful. If you sense a disturbance, then have a dialogue once again with your higher mind. Begin asking questions. If it is for your highest good to clear it away, then do it. Do this now. (Pause) Many people clear in different ways: Some visualize an eraser being used to remove what doesn't serve the greater good, some shower with colored light and wash the negativity down the drain, and others call in angelic or divine help to assist them with this process. There is no right or wrong way, your Higher Mind will show you the best way for you, because you do YOU perfectly.

After you feel complete from an etheric cleansing, ask your Higher Mind to do the same with your Astral Body. This is where you hold your emotions. As you know, this body can swirl with negative and positive emotions. It is not necessary to know where and why any negative emotion came to be, what is important is the release of any negative emotion for it can create havoc or ill health. You know this, so choose to be healthy. Choose to be happy. Choose to be emotionally well. Scan your Astral Body now. (Pause) Listen to the wisdom of your Higher Mind. Let your brilliant wise Higher Self show you, tell you, or help you become aware of what needs to be released for it doesn't serve you in anyway. Do this now. (Pause) Ask your Higher Mind to show you the best way to create harmony and balance between your emotions and physical body. Do this now. (Pause)

Choose a time in your life when you were happy. Happy with what you were doing, what you were contributing, or creating. Happy in relationship with a significant other, family, or friends. Happy in solitude with connection to God and receiving grace. Happiness is a birthright. Experience this memory as if it was happening now, right now. Allow the emotion of happiness flood your physical body. Allow your physical body to absorb and respond to all those happy feel-good chemicals in your brain. Say out loud "I feel good." "I feel happy." "I feel loved." "I feel complete." "I feel enough."

Good. You are doing so well. Now it's time to scan your Mental Body. Trust in the process for your Higher Mind will show you the way. You know what to do. (Pause) Ask, "What do I most need to know about my thoughts?" "Are there any self-limiting beliefs that I need to be aware of?" "What is the best way for me to clear these beliefs and also to remain steadfast with positive thoughts about self?" Begin dialoguing with your higher mind now. Affirm out loud with your own powerful positive statements. Do this now. "I am _____" "I am _____" "I am _____" Yes you are! (Pause) You know your thoughts are alive and reflect what you see in your outer world. Say out loud, "As I change my thoughts to the truth of who I am: a powerful beautiful and loving person, my circumstance changes. I am here for a reason. My thoughts matter because I matter. I shift my thoughts instantly if I regress to thoughts that do not serve my highest good. I know how to change, I know how to heal, I know how to love, I know how to serve. My thoughts are positive with focus and strong intention to the greater good of all.

I take a few moments now to express gratitude to all my bodies, including my spiritual body which helps me align with higher principles and purpose. I thank them all for the loving support, guidance and productivity that provided such a perfect vehicle for this present incarnation. I am grateful to all the living and unseen loved ones who continue to help me grow in love with self and others. Mostly I am grateful to God, my creator, who loves me unconditionally and is my greatest cheerleader."

Now it is time to come back to your full awareness. On the count from one to five I will count you up. One, you begin to notice the sounds and sensations all around you. Two, physically feeling well rested, wonderfully relaxed and yet a feeling of vibrant energy at the same time. Three, emotionally feeling very calm and centered, and greater love for self and others. Four, mentally feeling exceptionally alert, focused and wiser. And five, spiritually much more aware of who you really are; a loving soul who is here for a reason, with a purpose of loving and contributing in your own perfect way. You remember everything you experienced in this beautiful session. Choose now to either enter a blissful sound sleep for the evening, or to wake from hypnosis now. Wide awake or deep sleep. Your choice.

****

STRESS RELIEF

Take another deep breath, hold it, and let it out with a big sigh. Good. Do this again. And now another. It is your breath that helps you calm and relax when you need to. Long, slow breaths with a loud exhale tell your vagal nerve to calm rather than excite.

Place your left hand on your solar plexus, your gut. Breathe loving thoughts into this area of your body as you say, "I am safe, I am protected, I am loved." Breathe in your favorite happy color. Do this now. (Pause)

Using your mind, have a conversation with this chakra. Be a loving parent to yourself and say comforting words like "You are safe, you are protected, you are loved. It is safe to let go of any tension or pressure because you are relaxing. Your left hand has been gathering healing energy, and with your focused intention you channel this loving energy into your solar plexus. Notice the warmth or heat from your hand as it penetrates and relaxes you even more. The more you feel the relaxation, the deeper you go into relaxation. The deeper you go, the better you feel. And the better you feel, the deeper you go. Let the healing energy continue until you are ready to move your left hand to your heart and do the same.

Breathe loving thoughts into this area of your body. As you say, "I am safe, I am protected, I am loved" as you also breathe in your favorite happy color. Do this now. (Pause)

Using your mind, have a conversation with this chakra. Be a loving parent to yourself and say comforting words like "You are safe, you are protected, you are loved. It is safe to let go of any tension or pressure because you are relaxing. Your left hand has been gathering healing energy, and with your focused intention you channel this loving energy into your heart. Notice the warmth or heat from your hand as it penetrates and relaxes you even more. The more you feel the relaxation, the deeper you go into relaxation. The deeper you go, the better you feel. And the better you feel, the deeper you go. Let the healing energy continue. When you are ready, release your hand from your heart and place it in the most comfortable position.

As you become more and more relaxed, you are able to have a conversation with your Higher Mind. "I know I am human with various lessons I have chosen to learn. I understand it is my perception of events that brings upon a choice. I can either "react" or "act". If I react first, then my emotional ego will be stronger than my wisdom. Who do I need to listen to, ego or higher mind? Both are needed in different ways. My ego keeps me strong and determined to produce and act upon what I feel is important. It keeps my identity of who I believe I am intact. I need a strong ego to keep me grounded and protected. My Higher Mind has no ego. My Higher Mind is pure spirit and connected to God. My Higher Mind is wisdom, love, and everything my soul wants to attain. At any moment, I can choose. If it is for my highest good and others to react, then I will. If it is wiser to listen first to my wisdom within, and then act, then I shall."

As you say the words and ponder these thoughts, you notice you are no more distracted by the angst or anguish you previously felt. You moved into higher thought, away from conflicting emotions. You also realize that it is negative thoughts that keep you swirling and stuck in a soup of negativity. You always have a choice, again to "react" or "act" for you have free will. If you stay in reaction, who benefits? Perhaps temporary satisfaction for your ego, like eating a cookie to cool down a burning need of immediate comfort. However, if you have the discipline to stop and think, and then act, who benefits? YOU. You realize you can shift your perception any time you need to. You can choose to act rather than react. You can choose to be wise. You can choose to be kind. You can choose to be loving. You can choose to RELAX NOW and be present in this very moment; attentive to your heart's desire and wisdom within to make the best choice for you.

Now that you have chosen to feel connected to your Higher Mind, you feel different. You feel physically relaxed, mentally alert, and emotionally calm. You feel free. You show gratitude to your body and mind by smiling. Smile now and feel so much better.

Make a choice now whether to sleep for the night or wake up from this wonderful hypnosis and ready to continue with your day. Begin counting up from one to five, with each rising number feeling better and better. 1, 2, 3, 4, 5. Go to sleep or wide awake, make a choice.

****

SPIRITUAL HYPNOSIS

Notice there is a bench in this beautiful field of colorful wildflowers. Go to the bench and sit down. Ask for a bright white light to surround you as you call out to a being who loves you dearly.

A being who watches, protects and guides you. A being who supports your spiritual development and is thrilled to be with you at this time. Do this now. (Pause)

What does this being look like? Ask for a name. It just pops into your mind. If you don't receive one, then give the being a name. (Pause) It may feel like you are making it up, that's it is only your imagination. Remember, imagination is inspired information. Your brilliant mind receives guidance from your guides, teachers, loved ones, and most often your Higher Self telepathically. Who sits with you now on the bench? Do you recognize this being? Perhaps it is your Higher Mind. Whoever came is the perfect one for you to communicate with at this time.

Listen intently to what this beautiful being wants to share with you. Stay present absorbing the message until it is complete. (pause) If you have a question, ask it now and listen. You will either see the answer, feel, hear or know it. (pause) Keep dialoguing until you feel you have finished.

When you feel complete, thank the being and know that what you experienced was real, and always for your highest good. Ask for a sign from this being now. (pause) You will either be shown it visually, hear it, feel a sensation, smell or taste it, or have profound knowing. This is the calling card that awakens you to their presence. Do this now. (pause) You are never alone, and only a thought away.

In a moment I am going to count you up from one to five. You will have a choice to sleep deeply and blissfully through the night or become wide awake, fully refreshed and feeling terrific. Either way is a good and perfect choice. One, starting to become aware of your surroundings. Two, becoming more and more alert. Three, physically feeling deeply relaxed, and emotionally feeling so calm and content. Four, mentally feeling very clear, and five, spiritually much more aware of who you really are; a beautiful loving soul who shines bright. Make your choice now, sleep for the night, or wide awake.

****

PAST LIFE MEDITATION

Now that you have found yourself in a comfortable position, and in a place where you are undisturbed, close your eyes and tell your body and mind to relax. With your eyes closed, take three long slow deep breaths. Do this now.

Imagine you are walking in an art museum. There are many halls of paintings from different periods of history, and from different cultures. You have a choice to walk through hall one, two or three. Allow your wisdom within to choose for you. Do this now and begin walking down the hall. Look at the paintings that are hung at eye level.

One particular painting catches your eye because it seems to be painted in colors that illuminate or jump off the canvas. See the painting clearly. (pause) Hear what the painting says to you. (pause) Feel your emotions. (pause) Acknowledge your thoughts because you just know what you know. (pause).

You have a choice now. You can either jump into the painting to experience a scene or continue to observe the scene that appears in your mind's eye. Choose now. (pause).

Look down at your feet. What are you wearing on your feet? (pause). Feel your body, are you male or female? (pause). Examine your clothes and feel the texture. (pause). Are you inside or out? (pause). Are you alone or with others? Approximately how old are you? (pause). What is your name? It just pops into your head. (pause) What country are you in? (pause) What year is it? (pause)

What are you thinking about today in this scene? (long pause). What are your feelings about your thoughts? (long pause) What are you doing? (pause) Allow your imagination to expand this scene. If there is something that needs your attention, and if it is for your highest good, then continue here in this scene, discovering significant details. Begin by telling your mind what you are experiencing. Ask questions and have a dialogue with yourself. Do this now. (long pause) Ask, "Is there anything else that I most need to know?" If there is you will continue with the dialogue, if not let your higher mind move you to the next significant event in this lifetime. Do this now. (long pause) See it. Feel it, hear it, and know what you know. Keep dialoguing until you feel complete with the scene. (long pause). Ask, "Is there anything else that I most need to know?" (long pause) "Why is this important?" (pause)

Begin to bring your awareness back to the great halls of the art museum. Do this now. In the main hallway there are benches, and one specific bench is beckoning you to sit and contemplate. Take three long slow deep breaths. Do this now. You feel centered and calm. In this state of balance ask your Higher Mind the following questions:

"What is the connection between that life I just experienced and the one I am currently living in?" (long pause) "Why is this important now?" (long pause)

"What lesson do I most need to learn? Or did I learn it?" (long pause)

"What did that person who I was teach me?" (long pause) "How best can I integrate the teaching into my life now?" (long pause).

You are now ready to come out of this insightful past life meditation. You know a little more about yourself. When you are ready, open your eyes and smile. Acknowledge that your imagination is inspired information. Be grateful by thanking your Higher Mind for giving you this experience.

****

HIGHER MIND SPA MEDITATION

You have chosen the Higher Mind Spa to experience different aspects of yourself at this time in your development. Your Higher

Mind will show you exactly what you need to learn and grow. It is fun and multidimensional. Close your eyes when you are ready to begin this meditation. Allow all your senses to partake in this journey of self-discovery.

Imagine you enter into a beautiful building. The colors are soothing with beautiful paintings on the wall. You are greeted by a receptionist that offers you a cool refreshing glass of water infused with a fruit of your choice. The chair you have chosen to sit in is plush and comforting. You feel very royal as you wait to be called for your time in the rooms. Notice your thoughts. What are you thinking? (pause) Notice your feelings. (pause)

The receptionist comes back and smiles at you. She tells you to go to the shower. As she guides you to this room, a feeling of excitement starts to begin. Once naked in this gorgeous large shower, you turn on the faucet. Beams of colored light streams through the shower head instead of water. Different colors offering different types of cleansing for all your bodies; physical, etheric, astral, mental and spiritual. Anything that does not belong to you or does not serve your highest good is washed down the drain. One particular color is streaming down now. This is the priority color that you most need at this time. Take a moment to enjoy the sensation and rejuvenation. (long pause) When you are ready, close the faucet and put on a robe that is hanging on a hook. Feel the texture and notice the color of the robe. Leave the shower room and walk into the hallway.

There are many rooms. You will start with the first one on your left. Its name is written on the door – PLAYROOM. Walk in and close the door. Take all the time you need to experience the PLAYROOM. (very long pause) You will know when it's time to leave this room and go to the next one.

When it's time, go to the next one called the CREATIVITY ROOM. Walk in and close the door. Begin to see, feel, hear, and know everything about this room now. (very long pause) Again, you will know when it's time to leave and explore the next room.

When you are ready, go to the next room now called the HEALING ROOM. Walk in and close the door. It is important to take as much time as you need for you will be experiencing a healing on many different levels of your being. (very long pause). You will know when it is time to leave this room. If you need more time, stay.

When you are ready to go to the next room, VISITATION WITH LOVED ONES ROOM, go there now. (very long pause) When you are ready, go to the next room.

Walk in to the DEAD FAMOUS PERSON ROOM Here you can meet, have a discussion or ask as many questions as you want. (very long pause) When you are ready, the next room is waiting.

GUIDES AND TEACHER ROOM. Walk in and close the door. They have been waiting for you. (very long pause) You will know when it's time to go to the next room for you will be guided.

MY SOUL PURPOSE ROOM. (very long pause) Stay as long as you need. What is most important is the clarity you receive. When you are complete go back to the Waiting Room and sit in that comfortable chair once again. Reflect on what you experienced in this Higher Mind Spa.

Which room had the most impact? (pause) Which room energized your spirit? (pause) Which room gave you the most joy? (pause) Which room needs your attention now? (pause) When you are ready, open your eyes and if you want, journal your answers, and what you learned from each of the rooms.

****

LESSONS and MISSIONS: HOW AM I DOING?

You are now comfortable and sitting in a quiet place where you are free of any disturbance. Close your eyes and take three deep breaths to center yourself. (pause) Ask your Higher Mind to focus with great intention on your current progress with spiritual development. Your mind will show you a room where you can view, understand, hear, or participate in this quest. Do this now. (pause)

In this room there is a table with chairs. A large open book appears before you. Can you see it? What does it feel like? It is open to the page that you most need to know, for it answers the questions you seek. The left side of the page has a list of LESSONS. How many lessons are listed? Begin to read the first lesson, hear it or just know what it is. Do this now. (pause) Ask, "How am I doing with this lesson?" Let your mind create an instrument or scale of measurement. See, hear, feel or know the answer. (long pause). Continue down the list, repeating this process for each lesson on the page. When you are finished, thank your Higher Mind for giving you enlightenment.

Now you are ready to experience the right side of the page that holds your MISSION; your soul purpose and what you intended to accomplish in this present life journey. Allow the wisdom of the words to speak to you now. See, hear, feel, or know your spiritual truth. (long pause) Ask your Higher Mind, "How am I doing with my intended mission?" Receive the answer using all of your senses using the same instrument or scale of measurement. (long pause)

You will know when you are complete. When ready, open your eyes and smile. Place your hands on your heart and say, "Thank you for showing me what I most needed to know. I am blessed with awareness and grace as I move forward learning my lessons and accomplishing my mission. And so, it is."

****

SELF HYPNOSIS for CHANGE

Write down a list of five things you would like to make a change with. It could be anything. Your health, weight, finances, romance, career; anything is possible. If you can see it in your mind first, visualizing how you want it to be, you can manifest with self-hypnosis.

Choose one of the five. Which one on your list matters most? Which one is priority right now? Once you have chosen, it is time to write your customized script. Allow the thoughts to stream from your Higher Mind as you begin to write the changes you want to see. Make sure they are positive and in the present tense. Use words that include as many of your senses.

For example: For health: I see myself drinking 4 bottles of clean water every day. I can taste the coolness and it feels so refreshing. This cleanses and hydrates me perfectly. As I look at my watch, I see that it is 9:30PM and I feel happy as I turn off all electronic devices to prepare precious "me" time. I see myself meditating, journaling or reading in bed. I feel so comfortable in bed, and as I see the words start to blend, I know it is time for me to enter blissful sleep.

The examples above do not reflect the negative. If your first thoughts might be "I will not drink soda or anything with sugar." Or "I will not stay up scrolling through social media or watching tv." These statements have good intentions but your subconscious mind needs to recognize what positive thoughts and action are ideal. Think carefully as you craft your script. "Do not think of a purple elephant." Did you think of a purple elephant? "Think about a cute little dog or cat curling up on you lap to give you love and affection." Did you think about the little dog or cat?" You see the point now about writing positively.

Did you notice another mistake in the above examples? I said, "I will not..." instead of I am, I see, I hear, etc. "I will" indicates the future, a change that has not happened yet, or you are currently not doing. Your subconscious needs to be reprogrammed with your positive thoughts and experiencing it in the present moment, now. The word "will" is similar to "try". "I will try" usually doesn't manifest because you know what happens to your motivation and actualized plan when you think or say "try".

When you are finished writing your script in the positive and present tense, read it out loud. See where you can enhance the visualization with descriptive words that easily helps you visualize your desire. "Small white fluffy dog" describes a picture for your mind to see. Perhaps you want to see a scene in your mind as well. For example, shopping in a store looking through clothes with your ideal size on the tag, going in the dressing room and seeing how beautiful the outfit looks. Using your mind's eye this way is stimulating your clairvoyance - clear seeing.

Feeling the outfit as you wear those ideal size clothes uses clairsentience, touch and emotion. This is an important aspect of the process. Your subconscious mind needs to believe you are serious about this change your desire. "I feel how smooth the jeans feel against my body. The waistband feels comfortable and slightly loose. I am smiling as I look in the mirror because I feel confident and sexy and love these positive feelings I feel about myself.

Hearing is another sense that helps you manifest your goals in self-hypnosis. Hear your positive self-talk, "I hear my inner voice saying, "Good Job!" Hear others complimenting you. Hear the sounds of the environment of where you want to be. Clairaudience is your mind's inner hearing and it works wonders when you incorporate this sense into your magical script too.

Claircognizance is strong knowing. You don't know how you know, but you know what you know. It's absolute, ultimate reality. Capturing this sense in your self-hypnosis sessions is very powerful. Invite it in as you are using the other senses. Make what you are seeing, feeling and hearing real in your mind. Then you are truly knowing the soon to be manifested reality.

Your script is finished, and all that is left is the closing. This is a very easy part and you may find you don't want to end your session because hypnosis combined with your script feels so terrific! All you have to add is the following:

"Everything I have seen, felt, heard and know in my mind, is my truth. Each and every day and in every way, it manifests; easily and for my highest good. I am happy, I am grateful, I am confident.

On the count from one to five I will soon be in full beta consciousness. I need to make a choice when I say five to either relax into blissful sound sleep for the night or be very awake and energized. One, starting to acknowledge my surroundings and where my body is. Two, physically feeling so relaxed and very, very comfortable in my body. Three, emotionally feeling calm and centered, and yet a sensation of joy as well. Four, mentally feeling very focused and clear minded. And five, knowing I am capable and confident as my heart's desire is being created by my powerful mind and spirit. I am grateful and ready. Thank you. WIDE AWAKE, OR SLEEP DEEP. My choice, choose now."

When you are happy with your script, you can begin to record it on your phone. Start reading the induction out loud and read it slowly with the appropriate pauses. If you want to do a practice run before recording, this is fine.

Once you feel ready, the induction comes first, then your brilliant script followed by the closing. Listen to your customized script at least once a day. Your subconscious mind believes and changes the program through repetition. The more you use your self-hypnosis, the quicker and lasting the results.

Your mind is your most dynamic, influential secret power. It can help you or hurt you depending on how YOU program it. Choose your words, thoughts and deeds carefully. Ignorance is bliss, and you do not have the luxury to be fooled with naivety about negativity. You are human of course, and you will be triggered by other people and circumstances that happen. It is at these moments when you have a choice; to continue with hurtful thoughts or release them. Not bury them inside you, no. Rather making a choice to "act" instead of "react". And "Think before you act." This is tough in the moment, but so enlightening when you do it.

Your self-hypnosis script has given you many examples of how to replace "stinking thinking" with positivity. Use your visualizations, hearing and feeling to counteract the negative, and it will instantly raise your frequency. Your script is healing, and it heals you on many levels whether you are listening or re-experiencing it in your wakeful state. It is a gift that keeps on giving.

EPILOGUE

*W*hen we hear the famous words from Charles Dickens' book, A Tale of Two Cities, does it remind you of today? "It was the best of times, it was the worst of times, it was the age of wisdom, it was the age of foolishness, it was the epoch of belief, it was the epoch of incredulity, it was the season of Light, it was the season of Darkness, it was the spring of hope, it was the winter of despair, we had everything before us, we had nothing before us, we were all going direct to Heaven, we were all going direct the other way – in short, the period was so far like the present period that some of its noisiest authorities insisted on its being received for good or for evil, in the superlative degree of comparison only."

We incarnated in interesting times, haven't we? We each have a divine plan, a calling to activate NOW. Perhaps you were born to be an activist, healer, inventor, protector, teacher, guardian, mentor, artist, caretaker, leader. These are just some of the many roles we wear because it is comfortable to our soul. We have played the part before. It is your contribution and elevation of humanity that matters most.

The true stories and exercises in this book will hopefully ignite a spark of eagerness to explore your spirituality in a more insightful, personalized way. When you understand your true nature, your lessons and mission, you will indeed advance the evolution of mankind, including your own spiritual development.

My Dad used to say, "Are you here for a reason or a season? If you are here for a season, you are like a beautiful leaf that falls gently to the ground when the wind blows. However, if you are here for a reason, you have planted seeds that established firm roots to weather any storm. The tree is everlasting for you have made a difference."

Sure, we all get complacent in our comfort zones. We justify by saying to ourselves, "we are too busy, too old, too ill, etc. There are more important priorities to attend to." However, it is also important to recognize others who are experiencing trauma, tragedy, and loss. Using your innate gifts can offer much needed assistance. This is just one way to serve. Ask, "What is my way?" Listen to your inner voice, for your higher mind will show you the way.

It is time to be visible, kind, and mindful. It is time to step up and acknowledge your beautiful light. It is time for you to make a difference by just being YOU. Let love be your guide. Thank you.

AFTERWARD

I hope after reading this book, you are more aware of who you really are; an enlightened beautiful soul who is here to make a difference. It doesn't matter if you are doing something huge to save humanity, creating the latest and greatest, or listening deeply to a friend...Just being you, and just "being" is what matters most. When you are present in the moment, you receive the greatest gifts; awareness, signs, messages, and of course, answers to the reason why.

I hope you participated in soul discovery in Part III. It was easy and enlightening, right? Continue exploring for your journeys will always be different and new. Everything changes. If you want, you can do this with a partner, or small group who is also interested in spiritual development.

And if you would like to go deeper, you can host a live workshop with me. Gather like-minded friends to experience a customized online, local (if in NJ), or retreat in your area. Contact me at www.debrataubenslag.com or email deb@debrataubenslag.com for details and discussion on how we can make this happen for you. Another suggestion: The Reason Why makes a great book club choice. I am available as a guest author for your club too!

God Bless You, and all Whom You Love.
Warmly,
Deb

Thanks for reading! Please add a short review on Amazon and let me know what you thought!

ABOUT THE AUTHOR

Dr. Debra Taubenslag – The Transformational Facilitator

Dr. Debra Taubenslag is a renowned teacher, healer, and metaphysician with over 35 years of experience specializing in transpersonal hypnosis. She holds a Doctorate in Clinical Hypnosis and additional teaching degrees in Speech, Theater, and Special Education. A published author of numerous books, including *NO STONE UNTURNED: How My Special Needs Child and I Transformed Against All Odds,* has educated audiences worldwide, through unique metaphysical stage hypnosis presentations and retreats.

In her private practice, which began in 1987, Dr. Debra helps individuals discover their life's purpose and heal on a soul level through specialized techniques like past-life regression, life between-lives therapy, and mediumship to communicate with deceased loved ones and guides. Her work is grounded in a wide array of certifications and advanced training, including Neuro-Linguistic Programming (NLP), hypnosis for cancer patients, shamanism, vibrational energy healing, and psychic development.

Dr. Debra has also served as a faculty member, teaching hypnosis and massage therapy, and as a workshop leader at the National Guild of Hypnotists convention. She presents worldwide at corporations, holistic centers, and professional organizations, educating people about the power of hypnosis for healing and transformation. Additionally, she is a spiritual minister and an active member of the International Hypnosis Federation.

Her life's mission is to guide others in discovering why they are here and what lessons their souls need to learn, offering powerful tools for self-worth, and relationship healing through hypnosis.

Contact Dr. Debra Taubenslag
732-723-8083
Deb@debrataubenslag.com
www.debrataubenslag.com

Acknowledgments

I want to acknowledge and thank my husband, Dom, and my son, Nicholas. While in spirit, before we were born, we made soul contracts to be together again. You are both my inspiration and reason for my soul's journey.

To Susan Olak, marketing, web, and book publishing extraordinaire. Your multi- talented skills amaze me.

Cathy Philippou and Deb Muzik, my literary genius friends. Thank you for taking the time to read my first draft and make insightful edits. Your recommendations were very thoughtful and valuable. So grateful.

Julie Wright, thank you for creating a beautiful book cover that I love. You are an intuitive creative manifester!

Shelley Stockwell Nicholas, my personal cheerleader who kept me moving forward to finish this project. You are a blessing.

To my extended family and friends, here and in spirit... Thank you for listening, encouraging and believing in me. I love you dear ones.

RECOMMENDED HEALERS

Angelic Spiritual Guidance and Portraits: Rev. Donna Voll
www.angelstoguideyou.com/

Aroma Therapy and Essential Oils Educator: Marlene Leitman
LinkedIn.

Astrologist, Author and Teacher: Joseph Crane
www.astrologyinstitute.com

Biophilia Expert: Tammy Marshall
www.biophiliapharma.com

Healing and Wellness through Fascial Release and Love Retreats:
Maria Alfieris
https://magicalhandshealing.com/

Hypnosis Icon, Author and Teacher: Shelley Stockwell Nicholas
https://hypnosisfederation.com/

Sound Healing and Reiki Master: Joann Reinhardt   Facebook

Psychic Vibrational Energy Healer, and Creator of Sacred
Activators Card Deck - Marie Viola
https://www.marieviolaunlimited.com/

World Renowned Psychic Medium and Author: Joyce Keller
https://joycekeller.com

Book Club Discussion Questions

1. How thought provoking did you find this book? How did the book challenge or change your perspective or opinion on your own spirituality?

2. How did the book make you feel? Did it bring up any emotions? Which story and why?

3. How, if at all, did the book relate to your own life? Did it evoke any memories or connection for you with Spirit?

4. How would you describe the book in one sentence? What is the main message or purpose of the book?

5. What was the most memorable or impactful story in the book? Why did it stand out for you?

6. Did the book inspire you to take action, change your behavior, or think differently about yourself? Why or why not?

7. How did the author's story make you reflect on your own life and experiences?